T0131576

The Pain Sings a Song

SHALANDA SHAW

authorHOUSE®

AuthorHouse™
1663 Liberty Drive
Bloomington, IN 47403
www.authorhouse.com
Phone: 1 (800) 839-8640

Published by AuthorHouse 05/12/2015

ISBN: 978-1-5049-0096-6 (sc)
ISBN: 978-1-5049-0095-9 (e)

Library of Congress Control Number: 2015904133

Print information available on the last page.

Contents

Part II

This Is It

Part III
Inspiration

Part IV
Revenge

Part V

Revelation

Part VI

Transition

Sing!

Dedication

I would like to dedicate this book to my mother
for she has been through the ups, downs,
breakthroughs, walls, and success. She is my biggest
support. I love you mommy. You are the best.

My Mother

My mother
I admire
She does it all
And she does it well
She makes sure Shalanda is well
Mommy puts herself aside
And says, come here my child
My medication is out in the morning
I cry to her how much I feel down
And life's unwanted
She reassures me to live
Sends me on my way to program
With a big smile from cheek to cheek
Once again...
Because of her
Life wins!

If feeling down and out
Mommy calls out of work
Spends the day with me
And selflessly she loss the day's pay
To see her daughter happy and smiling again

I might have felt guilty about this
But Mommy
Reassures me
Nothing is more important than her daughter's
Happiness
So as I cry unhappily
Wish to die
Have suicidal thoughts
I remember my mom
And see her unselfish path

I try to live up to her standards
As suicidal thoughts
Knock on my door
Day in and day out
I choose to live
To see my mom's face more
As life with her is my
Unselfish way of giving back more

Preface

Recovery is a struggle; however, instead of this being understood and supported by society and our close loved ones, it is stigmatized. People need people to listen, and lend a helping hand. For, The Pain Sings a Song, therefore, take the time to snoop and help that family member or friend pouting in the corner. People do not be afraid to advocate, sing your pain. Do not hold it in, or be ashamed.

While I was diagnosed with a mental illness in my prime years of adolescence; life was a battle. It was like not being able to wake up from a bad dream. I was in denial. I had a refusal to believe what was at hand. Adapting coping skills, adhering to them, and achieving goals were at a dead end at one point in time of my life because of my mental illness such as bipolar disorder, borderline personality disorder, and post-traumatic stress disorder. I struggled to wiggle out of the room of denial and dance to the acceptance land where I clicked my feet and then had an awakening that it was time to take control and find my own way home by using certain coping skills. I first asked why? And I gave up on life, proclaimed that this was the life I had and it would never get better. I had distorted thinking. I was overgeneralizing. Therefore, It became the time to end it all because no one heard the songs I sang of distraught, anger, hopelessness, sadness, emptiness, worthlessness, fear, anxiety, discouragement, hypersensitivity, mixed emotions, low self-esteem, anger, rage, guilt, irritability, and thoughts of death. The song I sang was not good enough. But then inspiration came into the picture and this led to, "Revenge".

Revenge

It sounds so magnificent
Yet so bare
But daring
I want to get back bipolar disorder
For what it has done to me

So I smell revenge as sweet success
A poem everyday
Starting from August 1, 2012
I shall rise from the rubbles of pain
By putting it on paper

After working so hard at "Revenge", I had a revelation about my prognosis. It helped me to transition in my recovery where I still sing, but to a different tune. However, drawing from my own experience, I now listen to others. For The Pain Sings a Song and although words deny the help, a person's behavior signal that he or she wants a friend, *The Pain Sings a Song*.

The journey sings as I bellowed and yell from within a pain of utmost fear, hopelessness, feeling unworthy and like a burden. I sang as the trouble started in the midst of my popularity, and I began to lose my outgoing personality. At a ripened age of twelve years old I wasn't interested in friends, society or anything that anyone had to give. I locked myself in my bedroom and let the television take away my pain. I watched tirelessly. I watched religiously. With burgundy sheets over my light white flowing curtains, I hit the darkest note but felt joy again in my isolation with my television, my friend. I hurt badly but I couldn't put a note to it. I didn't understand why, but I felt the pain. The song I sang brought loneliness, suicide attempts, rage, anger, deep, deep depression, and mania. I had mood swings as if I was swinging from a tree, singing. When I swung up in the air I had the best feeling as if I had hit the perfect note but as I swung low, pain of deep sadness bellowed. I tuned to faith, therapy, hospitalizations, and medications. And this was how I was able to find peace as the pain sang a song.

Twelve

It all started at twelve years old
I started to withdrew from the love
Of those I knew
Feeling depressed
But I didn't know I was
Feeling lost
I kept a dark bedroom
I would smile away the pain
Of loneliness to anyone
It created a belief that nothing was wrong
So it all started at the age of twelve
When deep sadness
First called my name

I aged to fourteen years of age and so did my pain. Trusted into a new country, the United States of America, from Jamaica, I went through some dark times before I started to see the light. I reluctantly went to therapy sessions, and I neglected half of them. The song of pain I kept on singing, alone, and out of tune.

What is My Problem?

All I feel is anger
So all I do is shout!
Loud, loud, and louder
It only eases the pain for a short moment
So I know it is a bad outtake

I remember when I use to be out and about
But now I do is sit in a corner and pout
I hate life so much
So thinking of death
Gives me a sense of comfort

I hate to see the light
Darkness is what I prefer in my sight
I am losing my communication skills
Because I stay away from people
As far as I can and will

Suicide is on my mind
But I am told it is bad to do
Such a crime
I really like the idea of death
But to kill myself
Nah
I don't think I have the strength

It is much easier to frown than smile
Hmmm, I really have to wonder
Why?
I may smile sometimes
But it never really meets the eye
While others are content with sleeping tight
I am up all night
I try to sleep
But I always end up staring
At the walls and ceiling

I try to be happy when others are around
You have no idea how hard it is to carry out
However, as soon as they are gone
My comfort zone
I am able to renown

SHALANDA SHAW

I pursue two personalities
One is good
The other is a bad quality
At school, I am seen as an angel
However, at home I am seen as the child
That is working for the devil, overtime
I wish I could always be meek and mild
But that doesn't seem it will happen
No, not in this lifetime

Some say I am stressed
Others say I am way depressed
Well, whichever one it is, I don't care
All I know is that I have the desire
To be fixed
And I mean
Very quick!

But until I find my problem
And an explanation
I will continue to take antidepressants
As my medication
And being sulky
Will be my daily expression

After being diagnosed with Bipolar Disorder at the young age of sixteen I felt it was a friend and a foe. It was a friend when I had mania because I loved the natural high I felt. However, when I experienced anger and depression it became a foe. Therefore, that's how I end up seeing it as, "Bipolar Disorder: The Friendly Monster". It took me from soprano to baritone when I really want to find a bass in life.

Bipolar Disorder: The Friendly Monster

Bipolar Disorder
Nothing but a friendly monster
Tells you in life you will thrive
Suddenly it changes its mind
"See that pole? Drive!"

It befriends you with mania
Causes you to have a wonderful time
Nothing seems to be of danger
Because up and up goes the adrenaline meter

You have many thoughts in your head
While engaging others in a conversation
You talk fast and easily forget them
No need to worry though
It's quid pro quo
Just a little pausing
From so much intelligence

You have so much laughter
Life couldn't be much better
For everything gone bad
There's no reason to get mad
There is always a solution
No need to visit town of anger and confusion

Sitting there having a wonderful time
You have no idea of the brain's chime
Like a ghost on a creepy Halloween night
Boo!
Welcome to the pessimistic zoo
Click! Goes the lock
You are trapped

Depression has entered the cage

No way out

Here comes suicidal thoughts and rage

I want to die!

I'm nothing but a burden

Full of hopelessness and selfless worth

The only exit is suicide

Never mind though

I see exit life

Did I say I wanted to die?

No way, I said I have beautiful eyes

Mood Swings were taking over my way of life, my kindness to other humankind, and my drive to take life in hand and thrive. Every hour I had a different mood it seemed. I tried to be nice but if I was angry I would lash out. If I was depressed, there was no talking to anyone. And If I was manic I couldn't shut up or have a clue to do so. So anger, depression, and mania, were the three adjectives that made up, "Me, Myself, and I". In my own world singing, if only I could, soprano, tenor, contralto, it shifts; it's like hiding to sing in the shower. I am doing it a capella.

Me, Myself, and I

Sometimes I have to wonder
Why me?
What did I do to deserve such a disorder?
I have so many mood swings
I might as well build my own rollercoaster

Come aboard! I have plenty words to describe myself
Can you read? Can you define them?
Here goes! Enjoy the ride!
And please do, do have a wonderful time
Maybe you will, Maybe you won't
Who knows? Ain't gonna know until you join the boat!

I am enlightened
I am confused

I am on top of the world, feeling the best
I am six feet below the earth, in distress

I have positive dreams of the future
I see a knife, some pills, and a sharpened razor

With confidence I am built
I feel shame and guilt

I have magical powers to help others suffering
I pursue great ideas to kill myself
So that others won't have a burden

I can write good poems to exhilarate
I have better suicidal notes that will intimidate

Life is so great
It is a wonderful gift
I wish I wasn't born
Put me in the ditch

You are going up
You are going down
Isn't this ride profound?
Ready to get off?

Can't handle it anymore?
I know the feeling
Isn't Bipolar disorder appealing?
Yet reeling?

Time to exit the ride
I won't torture you anymore
I wish I could do that
To my brain, forevermore

I have to say I am jealous
Yet joyous and jubilant
For I am a special
Yes, a special little one

Developing the third stage of Bipolar Disorder had me in a bind emotionally and physically. For at times I was restrained to a bed to save others and myself. I was extremely strong, as in the hospital I lifted tables and chairs. It also took a lot of people to take me down. This was so because I was developing anger like no other and it was called, "Rage".

Rage

An unbearable pain of rage
My whole chest is red with anger
It is not mine
But my chemical imbalance's
And I don't have any way of expressing it
But through writing
I am now crying as I am writing
I've gotten two needles to sedate me
However, they still didn't have an effect on me
So I wallow in my pain
And I feel a void in my chest

To talk to mom
Oh I wish I was home
However, that day might not come
The rage is now gone
But it comes and goes
I can't deal with this anymore
Cut my neck
Put me eight feet in the ground

Anger was a demeanor I displayed first before depression and mania. It held me captive when I became angry for I said or did what would first come to my mind. I was very impulsive but then I would regret what was said or done later. I was out to hurt others that hurt me. I could not control it, anger was like hypnosis, "It Takes Over".

It Takes Over

Anger, Anger, Anger
It takes over
I am angry about many things
I need to detach some of the strings
For it only takes something little
To stick me like a needle
And it causes many problems
Leading to bad relationships with family and friends

I get angry
I show it right away
I'm isolated
And in my room I stay
Don't you dare talk to me
Silence, Silence, Silence
You, I don't see
My eyes are watery
They immediately dry up

Man, am I furious
It just builds up

Just like a volcano ready to explode
My lava: abusive actions and fiery words
Just burst
Words are annihilating
I'm in an argument
Let's take it up a notch
Don't you feel like physically fighting?
I am too caught up in the moment
What comes to mind?
Is immediately related to the tongue
It is only over
When I say I am done

The session is over
All I have now is guilt
What do I do with it?
Regret, Regret, Regret
Did I really say and do all those things
I am such a bad kid

I am still angry though
It wasn't right what they said or did
They caused my lava to overflow
Let me think
Hmmm, what should be their consequences?
What should I say?
Apologize or forgive?
No better yet, condemn
Hold a grudge, ignore them

I commonly had a feeling in my head that I attribute to the chemical imbalance I am feeling. It could be and it could not, but that is the best way for me to describe it, "The Feeling in My Head", perhaps, vocal weight?

The Feeling in My Head

So I have a feeling in my head
It feels like…
It feels…
It feels like…
Oh I know
If feels like liquids bouncing up and down
And all the way around

So that's the chemical imbalance I think
My head is displaying this everlasting confusing painful ink

If I did not take my medication?
I welcomed it
It is a bad rainy fally day?
I say hi to it
My medication is in the midst of balancing?
I might as well put up with it

Whatever may lead to it?
Oh I don't know

But I don't use it as an excuse to be mean
To not be clean
And lie in bed all day
It is just like every other symptom
Get up and play
For coping skills will pay the bill

So the feeling in my head
It is…
It…
It is…
Ummm…I know
A symptom from my illness
That could be easily fixed
By hard working coping skills
And some positivity

To foot the bill
I use my will

Sitting down I took a ride back in my history. I saw the mood swings I had. I saw how much pain I have felt. I also realized the impact I had on others and the effect they had on me. I made a list of my problems. However, I had aspirations as a result of Bipolar Disorder. To me it seemed beautiful. Therefore, I realized it made me who I am, "Shalanda". I was meant to do more than singing a capella.

Shalanda

A girl who is trying to overcome her problems
She was born with a mental illness
That didn't show itself though
Until she was 12 years old

Thoughts of killing herself
Thoughts of being golden
Thoughts of not eating
Thoughts of excessively exercising
Feeling hopeless
Feeling worthless
Feeling like a burden

Feeling angry
Feeling like the devil
Feeling like an angel

She attempted to kill herself four times
Each attempt following the one before
Proving to be more dangerous to her body
For her liver became seriously damaged

The fourth suicide attempt
She nearly died
Was comatose in the ICU
After her mom found her
On her bedroom floor
If another hour had passed by
She would have been dead
Sometimes Shalanda wishes that that was the end

See, Shalanda has a complex biochemistry
She has been on many meds
Some worked, some didn't
The ones that made her stable
Didn't last long, this made her worried
For it looked like it would soon be another trip to the hospital

In a year
Shalanda was hospitalized 6 times
It was helpful for her
But she thinks she would never have another trip there again
For to her, going there was failing her, her family, and friends
Moreover, she hated the bad experience

However, she knows she prefers that over breaking their hearts being dead

It's been almost two months that she was last in the hospital
And now her depression and mania is back
It's an improvement though
Because they aren't as extreme as the ones before

Now Shalanda try to take life day by day
And knows that depression and mania comes and goes
Therefore, the best thing to do is to talk to her journal, her mom, her therapist
Or whomever she trusts
She knows that obstacles are ahead
So being a little optimistic at times helps
Like knowing, she's going to be a great help to others
Because by then she would have been on both sides of the fence

I was feeling lonely as there was no one to beckon my pain to. Family awfully said things that hurt my feelings. Having no one to turn to and vent the pain, I felt, "Annihilated". Was I supposed to allow others to stop my singing?

Annihilated

Pushed to the ground
With words sharpened with hate
Meant to hurt
Single handedly kicked by flagrant actions
Felt like being thrown to the streets
By those "loving" ones around me
Mind filled with thoughts
That needs to be destroyed

Depression turns to anger

Why don't these people let me be?

Now and then I would like a hug
But it is filled with obligations
And empty promises
Nice words are rare
And getting bashed all the time
About clothes, hair,
And natural movements from the heart

SHALANDA SHAW

It is a game called unfair
I cry out, Help me!
And then I am told, "Back off bitch"
Laughed at and ridiculed
Who do you think you are?
They ask

We hate you
We don't want to go anywhere with you
Stay out of our room
Don't sit beside us in the couch
We are watching the television
And if you seem interested
We are going change the channel
And wait until you are gone

So I look into myself
Wondering how evil I must have been
Because these types of treatment
Annihilate my thoughts of joy
So I sit in a corner and cry
Fighting back makes no sense
Because then I would be
Coming out of my character
Leave it up to Jesus
I cry to Him,
But how much longer, Lord

I am being pushed to the ground
Almost reached six feet under
Please I beg You
I need a rescue
This is too much
For one person to handle
I am hurt
So they have succeed
In trying to annihilate my being
Later Diary
I know this chapter
Is nowhere near closed

No my dear
They have plenty more hurtful words
Because when I am done with this bitch, they say
She may add on another two more feet to her six under
I'll spit on your grave and smile, their actions comment
Later Dairy
They're out to destroy

Before the journey of living started I attempted to meet death. I contemplated the best way of dying to end my suffering. Life seemed like it was too much. I was angry and I took it out in poetry. I was angry at my family, psychiatrist, therapist, and anyone I crossed path with. To me death seemed like the best thing that would ever happen because the pain of living, the emotions I was going through; seemed too much for a seventeen year old. I had more to worry about than being cool in school or getting good grades. My plate was full and overflowing. I saw myself going but not coming. Bipolar Disorder was its name and it took me over. I showed mood swings constantly and I would not be afraid to start an argument because I was empty. I felt I was a burden to my family so I figured when I die; they should "Consider It a Favor".

The anger sang songs of despair, fear, anger, disappointment, low self esteem, and deemed suicide as means to end singing a capella; giving up my dreams of being part of a choir. But should I stop singing to please others, what about the joy to my ears the singing brings?

Consider It a Favor

Kin, Folk, and Kindred
It was the best and only good thing in my life
I had ever done
Putting you out of your aggravation and annoyance
And most of all to stop being such a burden
And such a big bitch
I did what I always wanted to do
Help others that are suffering
Consider it a favor

As for Kin
It wasn't your fault that I was always so guilty
I hated that I had you spending unnecessary money
And also for dragging you along with my mental problems
Causing all that pain
I was surely the daughter from hell
It was a wicked thing that I had done
Just do what you said you would,
"Cry for a minute and then move on"
I don't think though that I deserve a tear
For I was nothing but torture
Now you can have a peaceful home
There is no longer me to make it miserable

So be glad
Consider it a favor

As for my Kindred
I was truly a, "fatass", that was in your way
Now that I am gone I hope the passage is clear
I took out my anger on you two
It was wrong and now I regret it
Just like you have always said
"Without you we would have lots of fun"
And what even makes me see this as a true favor
In your own words, "I wish you were dead!"
What do you know now?
There are genies around
So continue believing in them
And please do as you said
"If you were dead we wouldn't even cry"
And believe me
That sure brings relief
Truth is I was thinking of haunting you
But then I think
Why would I bring harm to you again?
Bring misery?
That wouldn't be fair, it would be double cruelty
No need to worry though
You surely won't be seeing my spirit around

I would be gone for good
No, you aren't having a fantasy
Fairy Tales do happen
Do believe in them
Another way you could look at it
Consider it a favor

As for my Folk
You should be happy too
For there isn't any me around
To get you mad
You don't have to waste your breath shouting and cursing
Now I hope you use good words
Well in your case
I don't know what your reaction to this would be
For apart from the others, you didn't tell me
But if I were to guess
I would hope that just like I want the others to do
Just laugh
Consider it a favor

They say that it is selfish to kill yourself
But I say it is selfish to make others suffer because of your problems
Do not think that you all had anything to do with this
For you truly did the best you could in getting me help
I always wondered what it is that I was destined to do

I then figured it out
It played repeatedly in my head
"I need to be dead"," I need to be dead"…
Consider it a favor

I don't know if I should be sorry for killing myself
But I surely do know that I am sorry for causing all those
problems
I loved you all
Do what you didn't get to do when I was around
Have a great life
And remember
Consider it a favor

Wanting to make sense of my need to die, I tried to find a way to sincerely understand what I was going through. I wanted to find a reason when really there was none. So I wrote, "Explanation…Not". I tried to let others dance to my tune.

Explanation…Not

At first, I was not so sure
Because it would be nice to
See what the future may bring
I see no way out
I must kill myself
I can't take it no longer, of disappointing
Others and myself
I feel like such a failure
I have no future

As I sit here and write this
I am thinking what is the less
Messy way to be successful in my intent
See I was thinking of hanging myself
But there is no way to do that
Because the chandelier, I think
Isn't strong enough
Moreover, there is no, "safe", trees around
Then I think

SHALANDA SHAW

I can steal the pills my mom have captive
And swallow them one at a time when she
Does not know that they are missing
In addition, I would down them with some
Alcohol and some Benadryl
I had many others
But the desperate one would be
To stab myself in the chest and belly

I tried to kill myself three times before
They all took place in the summer of 2002 to 2004
One was impulsive
The others were planned
Only one nearly worked out
I was so mad when I woke up
In this world I was still around

Truth is, I am hoping to see a sign
To have some new reasons to live
I don't think it is going happen
Because all I see is darkness

Anyways, there is never a reason to do such a thing
Because it truly does not solve problems
It only leaves problems for the people
You leave behind

Lately, my head has been feeling weird
I know that I need a medication change or increase
Maybe that is a part of the reason for my intended action
The smart thing to do would be to tell my doctor
But like past experiences
I would be sent to the beloved hospital

See, I see myself as a cancer patient
They go through chemotherapy, radiation
And whatever meds and process to get rid of the cancer
It takes a while for something to work
Finally something does
The individual gets happy and hopeful
Suddenly, it doesn't work anymore
So it is like
Let us try something else
Just like before
Something works then stops
And the individual goes through this
Until they get to the point where
This is enough
It is too much
I am willing now to stop this procedure
And live the rest of the life I have
With my family and friends
I cannot waste it on feeling weak and unhappy on meds

Can you make the comparison to my problems?
Let me make it clearer

In my case, I have been on so many meds
Just like the cancer patient
Meds work and then they do not
I am sent to the hospital as a result
I am tired of this procedure
Therefore, I do not see the need to talk to
My family, friends, or counselor
I just do not see myself going through it anymore
You can say I give up
Moreover, just like the cancer patient
I know what can be the result
And I do not want it to happen
So I hope for a miracle

Well you might say that this is not a good comparison
But it is
Because cancer kills people
And the same thing bipolar does
Some people who have them end up dead
Cancer, homicidal
Bipolar, suicidal
Same result though
Dead, dead, dead

See what I mean? Maybe not
Nevertheless, to my point, I stand

Cancer is a disease that kills
Bipolar is too
Difference is, it tells people to do
What cancer by itself does
Kill, kill, and kill
And that is most likely the result of them two
Funny thing is that I prayed a lot and asked for cancer
I also asked for a murderer
But that's a completely new story

This is the end of my explanation
Wasn't it reasonable?...Not

At a very hard time of feeling lost and in my mood, I needed my kin's support and understanding. However, it was just as hard for her as it was for me, for she knew little about Bipolar Disorder. Therefore her judgments of my behavior kicked in viciously and I couldn't get her to comprehend so her reactions to things made it seem like she was, "Only Thinking of Herself". I tried to keep it at bass for I was talking about a respectful figure, but I was mad so it went to soprano.

Only Thinking of Herself

I can't believe my fucking Kin
I am planning to kill myself this August
I am sad about it and every time it plays in my head
I cry because I know that I don't really want to be dead

Anyways, today I got a letter from the College I'm going to go to
It said I have to take like four tests
I freaked out because there is no way
I am stable and ready to do it
It made me even wanted to kill myself more
I mean, what happened to the smart me?
Who use to be an eager student and taking tests
Was definitely not a part of my problems
In fact, my grades were the only thing I had control of

Until bipolar disorder completely took over

Now of course my control is anorexia

So, I said to my Kin,
"I got to talk to you"
I told her how I felt about the tests
And guess what the bitch said
"I don't want any more headaches from you,
You think it's going to be like high school
You have to know what you want to do, you know what,
Just stay home."

She was vicious and mean
Not only what she said was upsetting
But her tone, my gosh
This bitch is so misunderstanding

Here I was trying to reach out to her
Thinking that she had change her nasty
Reactions to things I tell her
As a result, I felt guilty
I told her, "Bye, bye",
"Get out of my room"
She wouldn't leave
So I went and locked myself in the bathroom
I cried and cried

SHALANDA SHAW

I felt crushed
Trapped, alone, mad, lonely
Sad, more depressed, more suicidal
Hopeless, and relieved
This bitch would truly be happy if I was dead
Only thinking of herself

I had only complain about fears of tests
Could you imagine how this bitch
Would react, if I said I am planning to kill myself
Let me guess, I know I hit this one right on the nail
She would say
I don't want any more of your problems
Always giving me headaches
I am tired of you
I'm going to send you to Jamaica
Go there to kill yourself
You better don't do it
Because all you are going to do is
Bring shame to me and my family
End of reality quote

She the pattern here
Every problem of mine she turns into hers
It's her, her, and her
She does not think about how I feel
And how she must choose her words carefully

How about saying

I am sorry you feel that way

Let us talk about it

Why do you want to kill yourself?

Would you feel safer in the hospital?

What is it that you want me to do about this?

Please don't do it

I love you and would be in terrible sorrow

If you did it

Think about your future

You are very smart and I see

A lot is going to happen for you

End of fantasy quote

Do you see the difference?

In the latter words

This Kin cares about her daughter

And tries to reach out to her

Encourages her to live

And gives her reason

If only Kin could take a page out of that book

But no

Only thinking of herself

Anger was tearing my wits apart. I wanted to show everyone who I felt did me wrong, the famous middle finger. Why all this pain and anger? I felt stigma from my family. Also, I felt ignorance surrounding me, my doctors and therapists who was in charge of my care at the time. I wanted them all to know, "You Know What...Fuck You". I sang aloud with passion, with anger lashing.

You Know What...Fuck You

To my Kin, Kindred, Kindred, and somewhat counselors
See, I was in a lot pain
I couldn't really talk to anyone
But who gave a fuck anyways
I was sent straight to the fucking hospital
I couldn't truly talk how I felt
Responses were, "I don't want any more of your problems
From the day you were born
You were a pain, trouble, and nuisance
Brought aggravation and lots of problems"
"We are worried about you and your safety
I mean, hello, is anyone fucking listening
I said, "I am suicidal but I don't have a plan"
I just wanted someone to trust and to talk to
Without being threatened to go to some
Group home or a fucking hospital
Is anyone fucking listening?

I said, "I am suicidal but I don't have a plan"
You know what…fuck you

I wasn't able to talk about my problems
Because what do you know
I became guilty because of some people's response
I was afraid of being sent to the fucking hospital
I stayed in my fucking room and watched a lot of television
But no one was kind enough to take me out of the darkness
and lend me a hand
I cried a lot and I couldn't share it with anyone
People I was around gave me mixed signals
I wondered, "Do they love me?"
No they didn't
Because all the times they expressed
The joy they would have when I am dead
Satisfied now?
You should be
You know what…fuck you

What did you know
I had bipolar and became anorexic
Tired of being bothered,
"Did you eat?"
It's my fucking mouth and I control
What goes in and maybe come out
See my friend, Ana

Gave me control
Something in my life, I had to do
Because finally I had domination
Something at last gave me power
"Hunger hurts but starvation works"
But then arise another problem
I hated what I saw in the mirror
I couldn't share that with anyone
Because surprise, surprise
I would be off to a fucking institution
My life was becoming out of my hand
I felt in the unknown
All I saw was darkness
Wished someone could help me see the light
Nevertheless, that again I had to keep to myself
Why?
Well, what do you know?
It would be another trip
To the beloved hospital
You know what…fuck you

See I remember when I started eating again
Guilt followed me and my suicidal problems
I didn't have a plan
However, in front of the dishwasher I sat
With a knife to my chest

I wanted to stab
Crying, I felt alone
I didn't exactly know what I should do
Then I thought to myself
This august I shall be dead
No one listened
So at last
I was suicidal and I had a plan
Happy now?
If I am not dead by then
It would be a fucking miracle
You know what…fuck you

See as you can tell
I wrote this poem in anger
But just like the mean things you always say
And then said, "I didn't mean it"
"You know I love you right, I said it out of anger"
Who gave a fuck?
You knew my condition
I was hurting and fragile
You know what…fuck you

Well look at this poem that way
I wrote it out of anger
So maybe I didn't mean the mean things I said
Who cares?

Ain't sorry for you....Boo Hoo
You know what...fuck you

Can't say I didn't live up to my middle name
"Bitch!"
Been called it so often
I believed and acted like it
Although sometimes I would say kind words
I received resent and curse words
Tired of this shit
You know what...fuck you

I always felt like I wanted to die. I also felt I needed control. So not too longer after being diagnosed with Bipolar Disorder, I turned to anorexia. I had two strikes to count me out of the game of life and I loss the will to fight. I just wanted it over and so I was, "Tired". My voice became shaky so I wanted to stop singing.

Tired

Tired, tired, and tired
I am just tired
Tired of feeling like I am a burden to my family
Tired of feeling guilty
Tired of being sad and hopeless
Tired of being helpless
Tired of feeling lonely and being alone
Tired of isolating
Tired of taking trips to the hospitals
Tired of an ever changing prescription
Tired of being worthless
Tired of thinking about death and suicide
Tired of hearing a tape playing in my head
What I should write before committing suicide
Tired of researching ways to kill myself
Tired of being impulsive, saying things
When angry and then later regretting them
Tired of being angry

Tired of feeling confident then hopeless in a second
Tired of praying for cancer or a murderer
Tired of seeing nothing to achieve
Tired of living in fear of school
Tired of being, "high", and then depressed
Tired of crying
Tired of hating spring, fall, summer
Tired of seeing my scars
Tired of putting on makeup to cover them up
Tired of seeing my fat
Tired of starving myself
Tired of weighing myself everyday
Tired of hating what I see in the mirror
Tired of looking at pro-anorexic websites
Tired of feeling guilty after eating
Tired of hating myself
Tired of thinking what my weight should be
Tired of thinking how many days and weeks
I'm going to need to achieve it
Tired of exercising
Tired of lying about what I've eaten
Tired of people asking

Tired of comparing myself to others
Tired of thinking they are slimmer or better than me

There's no way someone could have helped me

It's sad, sad
That I had to go this way
Because on this earth I wanted to stay
But I felt trapped
I was in a dark hole
My hand was trying to dig me out
However, the space for my escape wasn't big enough

In the midst of starving myself for fifteen days my mom found out and demanded that I eat. However, I loved the emptiness I felt in my stomach waking up in the mornings because I didn't eat. So knowing I won't have those feelings anymore if I started eating again to my mom I was asking, "Please". I didn't have the fuel to keep going but I had to prove otherwise, so soprano was frontline.

Please

Please let me starve myself
I promise I won't die
I just want to be perfect

Please let me starve myself
I promise I'll start to eat
As soon as my goal weight is reached

Please let me starve myself
I promise I'll make food my friend
And no longer an assailant

Please let me starve myself
I promise I'll like what I see in the mirror
Because after this I'll be a guilt free eater

Please let me starve myself
I promise I won't weigh myself everyday
And my exercise routine will be moderate

Please let me starve myself
I promise it will make me happy
Because vain and controlling has become me
And I hate and love it

A plea made to family members and friends of consumers who have bipolar disorder to help out, and be more understanding, for one can't just snap out of it. It is an illness and consumers need support. It is through the help of others that makes the battle easier if they "Share the Bipolar Load". I go on my Knees and belt it out, like I never before, from the stomach, I roar.

Share the Bipolar Load

So you have a loved one
With Bipolar Disorder
They get depressed, manic, and angry
They sometimes take out every inch of problem on you
Isolating
They don't want to talk to anyone
All of what is on their mind is the will to die
Then happiness has suddenly arrived
They are feeling the best
And they can do any or everything
Then suddenly it turns into rage
They will argue with you from morning until noon

Now that you've gotten just a little
Peek in at an individual's bipolar show
Try to put yourself in their shoes
Encourage them everyday

Help them out of the depression, mania, and rage
It will be gladly appreciated
It is not entirely their fault
It is the illness talking
Love and cherish them too
They are also humans
And Bipolar disorder may be the diagnosis
But it is not them too

A lot of people in the world have their own ideas of mental illness which are misconstrued and ignorant. Therefore this is a poem to shout out that being mentally ill does not make a person crazy but rather challenged in their daily life and reiterate that comprehension from a third party is welcomed. Hands in the air, eyes open and focus, look at me, promise me, you give up, sing, soprano everyone, "Say No to Stigma".

Say No to Stigma

?Crazy?

!Challenged!

Mental Illness is OUR

Forum

Recovery is OUR

Token

Living is OUR

Right

Stopping Ignorance

Is OUR

Fight

Educating one by one

Is OUR

Light

To end stigma

And to live freely

For we are not crazy but challenged daily!

I have been diagnosed with bipolar disorder and I have experienced its dangers. However, my fear is that I am not respecting God. As my faith grows stronger in Him and I get better daily, my reason for living comes from Him, the one I fear, "It's God". I take it down, all the way, on my knees, bass.

It's God

God
It is You, I fear
My mind battles the questionably pain
Why, I have to ask
Why?
I developed an illness
It turned me to You
I sought to understand through Theology
I was so confused
I didn't understand how I am so smart
And may I add, beautiful
Yet I feel incredibly intelligent
Ambidextrously stupid
And a classic fool
Christian schools are no longer my forte
And going to church is no longer my stew
The Bible is smiling shut
Yet I feel so close to You

SHALANDA SHAW

I feel Loyal
So yet again
Am I
Am I confused?
Not this time
Wondering what to do
But oozing with proudness
I see
With hard work and dedication
I can do anything
Therefore, God
It is You, I fear
It is now clear
Life may be unfair
And as it bullies me
I take the high road to positive thoughts
For
It is...
It is ...
You, I fear
God
Yet you are always there

There was a time when I was feeling deep in the darkness and feeling lonely. It was time to use my coping skills of writing and find the light by understanding I was, "Unhappy". I am forgetting the words, but I still push to sing.

Unhappy

I am so unhappy
I get hungry
But when I cry
The tears full my belly
Why Lord?
Why are you putting me through this?
I can't run to kin or folk for help
And I can't talk to Tom, Dick, or Harry
I need to break free of this prison
I don't want to speak anymore
All they do is hear
No one listens
The pain is overwhelming
I can't take it anymore
Why Lord?
I am drowning
I need floats
I can't swim

SHALANDA SHAW

As a matter of fact you taught me how to swim
But I forgot
So I can't swim anymore
Therefore I come to you in prayer
Begging you, please
Help me!
Take me out of this darkness
And it is like I am talking to a board
They curse me out
Turn their backs to me
Yell at me
And provoke
They don't listen to my pain
Or even notice it
They mistreat me instead of treat me
Why am I here Lord
Lord, please
Help me!
I can't take this
If only I could hear Your voice
It would just soothe me
Why Lord?
Please
Help me!
I am suffering

A plea I made to those around me when I was drowning in painstaking depression and darkness. I needed them to help me and, "Listen to My Cries". As I sing, tears flow down the cheeks but nonetheless, I sing.

Listen to My Cries

Yes it is my diagnosis
But I try to work as one with it
I am tired of crying spells
I am tired of thoughts racing through my head
Furthermore, when hastily talking I easily forget them
I am tired of crying alone in the dark
And not seeing a hand stretching out
To pull me out of the depths by grabbing my hand
And saying it is going to be all right mam
I am tired of sleepless nights
There is no one to talk me out of misery
I am tired of feeling depressed
And also feeling like I want to commit suicide

Please someone help me
Listen to my cries

I used to be ashamed of my mood swings and intensive emotions. However, now that I have matured and I understand the illness more through therapy, I express my feelings through writing, I, "Let it Out!". While singing I place emphasis on the words related to my feelings.

Let it Out!

I scream out
Do they hear me?
Please
Can somebody love me?

No friends
Feels like
I have no family

Hit with harsh words
Broken down
I screamed out

What did I do wrong?
Why all this pain?
Why all this hate?
Why silence?
Why break?

Beauty and smartness lurking
But stroked out
With Bipolar Disorder
I met stigma
She was very
Very thirsty

I cry
I hate
I bait
No one likes me
I feel counted out of the game

So I figured how to like pain
Before it swallows me

Let it out!
That's me
No shame

I was feeling pain out of my unstableness in moods. I was in the hospital and I wanted to go home but at the same time I needed to be there to get better. However, I was in a place, frustrated, where only God had the answers to my fear, low self-esteem, and wanting to end it all. Therefore, I turned to him saying, "Nobody Understands But You". I did not have the strength to stop singing myself so I wanted God to stop me instead.

Nobody Understands But You

Nobody understands the cries I've cried
Nobody understands the darkness I am in
Nobody truly understands how I feel
Nobody understands why I want to end it all
Nobody understands why I hate me
Nobody understands why God saved me
Nobody understands but You Lord
So take me now
I beg of you
Please!

Being in the hospital for a long period of time can be bittersweet as old consumers leave and new ones are admitted. Therefore, this is a poem to help inspire others when challenges are faced and to keep our heads up as personality clashes when consumers are, "Cycling In and Out". I sang wherever I went.

Cycling In And Out

Things are changing
Old ones are going
New ones are coming
It is hard
For one has to hear it from doctors, fellow consumers, and staff
Also our loved ones on the phone
It is not always a positive transaction
However, all of that does not matter
Only YOU come first
So they may bite you
They might pinch you
They might stab you
And kick you down with words
But as I have learned
They are only words
Don't let them pierce your membrane
You are in the hospital to work on your mental illness

SHALANDA SHAW

So huddle in bed tonight
And avoid
The trick or treaters of the brain
To all, have a goodnight
It is possible with all your might

Falling on hard times of being ill, the only way to help myself was to go to the hospital. Furthermore, although I understood this logic I was tired of being admitted to psychiatric hospitals, therefore at this point in time I needed to be in the hospital. Because of the vicious cycle I was in then, my thought was, "Here We Go Again". Although I was forced to sing the same songs I accepted the repetitions and kept on singing.

Here We Go Again

Here we go again
Another trip to the hospital
It is definitely not my friend
So I cry because I do not want to go
I know I need the help
But to be gone for fifty days?
That seems like a waste
It is not at all
For it is the next step in recovery
It just feels like my family willingly committed me
It seems they have control over my life

Beneath these four walls
Doctors will seal my fate of departure
I feel ostracized and so left out
I just want my family to understand

SHALANDA SHAW

I love you all
But it is not every single problem
That I should be in the hospital for
Please, let me breathe a little
And take my medication
Use my coping skills when necessary
But here we go again
Bellowed these words
You put me here
I am back in the hospital again

Going to hospitals became second nature as I was seriously ill. However, at times seeing the same walls and having restrictions to going outside, I was tired. I wanted freedom so that created, "Another Episode of Tired". My voice was shaky all over again but for different reasons; however, the singing continues.

Another Episode of Tired

I am tired
Tired of being in these hospitals
Dang it
I am brewing with anger now
A girl can't catch a break anywhere
Man, am I angry at everything
I want to leave
And I mean right now
Get me out of here!
I am tired, ANGRY
I am confused
I need Jesus in my stew

I am very sorry Lord
Thank you for your forgiveness
I shall be a great example
Through and Through
Now that you have thrown tired out the door

With everything seeming out of control after a diagnosis I felt a relief of pain. I needed something to make me feel better so I turned to, "Control". I liked being in charge of the songs I sang and the notes I sang them in, so for that reason I was encouraged to sing.

Control

I've controlled many things
Getting good grades
If and what I should eat
And when and how long should be my exercise routine
My feelings, so that to others
I won't be vulnerable
If I should isolate and pout
Or talk to friends and hang out
Give in to my depression and attempt suicide
Or try coping skills until it subsides

Control is something I have to have
Without it I tend to be suicidal
Need something to give me power
Need something to make me worthy
Need something to make me feel like a worshipped flower
Need something to make me happy
Need something to make me eager and desire
So control is what I require

It is a good feeling to think that I could be in control of my reactions to my mood swings and suicidal thoughts. Therefore, with this positive attitude in mind, I believed that, "It is Only over When I say it is Done". I sang the songs and I loved the idea that the singing stopped only when I said it was time to stop.

It is Only Over When I say it is Done

It is only over when I say it is done
I might get a mood swing
So I curse you out instead of using my coping skills
So, it is only over when I say it is done

I may have suicidal thoughts
But I am going to kick in the positive ones
It is only over when say it is done

I may curse you out with anger lurking
But I have control
So it is only over when I say it is done

I may decide to lockup my problems and hold the key hostage
But I will talk about it in therapy
So that it does not lead to a possible suicide attempt
So, it is only over when I say it is done

So, I say to you
Do you have control?
The depression is binding
Are you going to use your coping skills?
I must ask

Is it only over when you say it is done?
Latch on?
Let go?
You are in control
Talk?
Fight?
Use the coping skills?
Swallow the pills?
Partially
It is only over when we say it is done

Being a patient in a psychiatric hospital there are many rules to adhere to that will ensure one's release. If one goes against these rules then life in the hospital will be prolonged or one would be sent to another hospital that is long term, lasting for six months or more. Therefore to avoid this I obeyed the rules and, "Sing to Their Tune". I like my own way of singing but there were times when singing another tune was all right in doing.

Sing To Their Tune

La la la la la
La la la
La la la la
La la la la la la
I could sing forever, because I have just been given
My release date from, "prison"
So today is Thursday
And things are going my way
Whoo…
I am feeling like hot pepper
If you step on my toes
I guarantee you a third degree burn
Smile
I am just kidding
La la la la la
La la la

La la la la

La la la la la la

Did I say I feel like singing

I love you all

Thank God

I wish you the best in battle

See you all on the outside

I'll try to keep my mouth

Ill-filthy

And try to be nice to the doc, docter, doctor

Whatever you call him or her

Next week, my darling

However, meanwhile

Let's sing

La la la la la

La la la

La la la la

La la la la la la

Let me let you in on a little secret

Shhh…

Listen up

If you sing out of tune your stay will be prolonged

Don't be sad though

Just keep on singing

Because if you believe

In tune you will definitely sing

SHALANDA SHAW

La la la la la
La la la
La la la la
La la la la la la
My job here is done
Hahahahaha
They are going to let me out
Hahahahaha!
Sing!

The hospitals experiences aren't just sad times. There are a lot of times when there is a funnier lighter side, especially when I had a, "Competition" with "Chelsea". Five dollars is the reward. Who will be the winner? Who can hit the highest note?

Competition

"Chelsea" and I are in a competition

Who can keep their feet high off the ground for four minutes?
Five dollars is on the line
And "Chelsea" wants to win it, badly
So the clock is going
Tock, Tock, Tick, Tick, Tick
Just watch
Two minutes to go
Tick, Tick, Tick, Tock, Tock
I just love this hospital
"Chelsea"
Here we go
We are down to seconds
I could stomp those feet to the ground
However, we have a winner
"Chelsea"!
She stuck to the bet
Dang it, there will be a next time
I am going to get my five dollars back
That's what I'll dream about tonight…hahaha

Just sitting and thinking, I wondered what life might have been if I had comprehended fully the days ahead having bipolar disorder. Would I be more prepared? Would I have fewer hospitalizations? They are the questions I ponder and more, as I ask, "Did you...Have you?" Soprano?...Bass?

Did you...Have You?

Did you ever grow up thinking,
You are going to try to commit suicide some day?
Have you ever thought that you are going to have anger,
That tripped you so badly?
You could take down a seven feet tall guy, proudly?

Did you ever grow up wishing that you would have multiple,
Psychiatric hospitalizations?
Did you ever grow up wishing that you could,
Switch moods in a matter of seconds?

Have you ever thought that going through these motions,
Society would close the door in your face,
And wouldn't give you a hand?
Did you ever wish that you were happy,
And never knew the word depression?
For it holds you in a darkness
That makes you feel you are cushioned

Have you ever as a child wish that u would feel,
Caught in a net with extreme emotions?
Did you know that you would threaten your life,
Have it lingering in your own hands?

Did you ever...?
Have you ever...?
No you haven't
Because we all grow up wishing to be a firemen,
Policemen, lawyers, and doctors

The positive list goes on and on
Since you didn't or haven't thought of such things
I say to you
Now that you know
What are you going to do?

Life can be so tiresome and dreary when symptoms are in control and it feels like it took over our joy for life and leaves us just wanting to give up and die. Therefore, to bring back joy and get rid of pain I encourage you, "Don't Give Up, Keep Going". I just can't seem to hit the high notes but I don't give up, I keep trying. I will get it one of these sweet days.

Don't Give Up, Keep Going

It may seem you may be cowered under trees
And the breeze is coming just for you
And it is blowing hard
But you hold on tight
Just don't give up, keep going

Don't give up, keep going
You are so depressed
You feel like you are actually in your grave
But not totally
So you think you should do something
To get to your final resting place
But then the wind blows and your curtains open
And you see light
That's God saying hi
He hasn't forsaken you
Don't give up, keep going

Have you heard voices calling your name?
But you get scared and resist
With that little bit of strength in you
That's your will to live
Don't give up, keep going

Have you ever wanted to commit suicide?
Feeling like swallowing those darn pills
Feel like jumping over that darn bridge
Feeling like cutting your darn wrist
The list goes on and on
But you don't
Because of future goals
Don't give up, keep going

So to end it all
Not your life of course
But this poem
Keep going strong
Just don't give up, keep going

Wait, there is more!
Don't give up, keep going

With our illness
We have them
They don't have

Or define us
Life is a recovery
You can do it
So please press on
When problems knock at your door
Kick them down
Don't answer them with a smile
Smile after the job is done

Thank you,
And remember,
Don't give up, keep going
Press On my cute little ones
The job has just began

Being diagnosed with bipolar disorder I did not only invest in its symptoms but I also faced the stigma that came from people around me. I was no longer the Shalanda they saw and knew. I was different in their eyes. Therefore, because I know I was still me, I had to ask, "How Did It Get Here"? How is it that I sing beautifully high pitched or dreadly low and the crowd disappears?

How Did It Get Here?

How did it get here?
We drifted apart because
Suddenly I developed a mental illness

How did it get here?
My love for you is still here
But you no longer want anything to do with me
Because of fear

How did it get here?
I understood what you were going through
But you didn't even lift a finger to clue in on my blues

How did it get here?

I told you I love you
But you say
You only loved me for what I was back then
Why fool?

How did it get here?
I accepted these problems and obstacles
But you pushed me aside

I know how it got here
I now have bipolar disorder
And you ran off to be with sane
Because you claim
I am now different
What a shame

If knowing when bipolar disorder would enter my life from birth, I felt I could spare my family and I from the rough journey ahead by being more prepared. But there is not such a thing, therefore instead of wishing for the impossible I should go by what I know now and not coveting, "If Only I Knew". If I knew that you would hate my singing I would spare you but I can't stop singing, no apologies.

If Only I Knew

If I Only Knew
That I would be diagnosed with Bipolar Disorder
I would save you the pain ahead of time

They come my way
Depression, hopelessness
And feelings of worthlessness

If I only I knew,
I would try stop hating me too
If only I knew
I would have warned you
Of my mood swings
If only I knew
I would have told you to be prepared
For I may want to make suicide attempts
If only I knew

SHALANDA SHAW

My darling
I would spare you of my brew

Please accept my height
I have Bipolar Disorder
And I love you
With or without it

If I only knew
I would protect you too

Feeling isolated by others and it was not my own choice, I needed attention and love other than the love I knew from up above. I wanted to be seen and not ignored. This brought about a drive to love others and give back. As a result I had a void I was out to fill and because I desperately wanted to do this, my heart was, "Hungry". I want to draw a crowd in with my voice but they are not coming.

Hungry

I am hungry
Hungry to feel loved
Hungry to share
Hungry to pass on the Lord's loving
Hungry to give
Every ounce of my body
Hungry to stop feeling lonely
I want to hurt someone as much as they've hurt me
I want to get rid of hate and their dead promiscuity

I am angry and Angry and angry and angry and Angry I say! say
Why am I so damn angry?
Hmmm… let me see
I am hurt and Hurt and hurt and hurt and Hurt I say!
Now why am I so hurt?

Hmmm…let me see
I love and Love and love and love and Love I say!
Now, why would I love?
Hmmm… let me see
I figure it is because
I give and Give and give and give and Give I say!
Now, why would I give?
Hmmm… I am a damn fool to do such a thing

I am angry because they hurt me
After loving them and giving them thoughts of the heart
I ask, should I still love?
Yes, definitely
I am not about to let them win
I claim victory to the end
And you may hate
But one day I know you'll be a friend

I was wondering if all these bad experiences were true. The feeling of loneliness and on top of that, neglected, ignored, and floored by harsh comments from my kin, folk and kindred. But despite their negativity I still overcame. I accepted what was happening because it shows my growth. So out of disbelief because of everything I wondered, "Me?" Why shouldn't I sing?

Me?

Kin do you hear me?
Folk do you know me?
Kindred I am sorry
Why are all these fingers pointed at me?

I have been diagnosed with Bipolar Disorder
Yes
But I am still here
Could you please love me?

Why can't you speak to me?

What bad did I do?

I remember being together as allies
Reminiscing about our childhood in Jamaica

Now that bipolar said Hi

And I unwilling befriended it

You

You forgot me

I'm screaming beneath these mood swings
I am still me!
Bipolar disorder does not defy me!

Why
Why all this hate

WHY all this PAIN
Plus loneliness
And fear

Hate fueled by stigma
Pain lingers
Loneliness instills
Fear bewitched

Driven by success
I know
I
I can be my best

Feeling

Kin cannot hear me
Folk do not know me
And Kindred will not forgive me

This is a time to succeed
For I might not hate back
But success is revenge

Succeeding to teach
Succeeding to help others believe
Succeeding to diminish stigma

Feeling to make sense of my pain
Feeling like triumphing hate
Feeling like dancing on water
When I should be sinking
I am smiling

For

Kin should listen
Folk should accept me
And
Kindred can learn to do better

But although they don't

I

I still triumph

Because I

I

Love me

Beneath these tears of why
I came to the conclusion of
Why not me?

After being in self-pity asking a lot of whys until there was no more to holler I had an epiphany and I realized, Why not me? I should accept the challenges of singing in the beginning because with practice it will become easier.

Why?

Why does it hurt so much?
I feel abandoned
I try to talk to my family on the pay phone
And all they do is yell at me
I try to talk to staff
However, the one that truly understand is God, and me

Why do I have to suffer like this?
See these scary things that doesn't really exist
And I hear these voices that repeatedly call my name
Why do I have to believe there are cameras among my surroundings?
Watching
My every move
When it is not true
Why do I have to experience this storm now?
I want to be in the calm of the eye
I am so ridiculed and talked about
Why, oh why?
You know what I am going to turn it around

Why not me
I am special
That's why my obstacles are harder to climb
And the sweet success at the end
Is sweeter than candy
For I have again made it over the hurdles
So, Why?
I'm a beautiful butterfly
That can overcome a rocky flight
And because the harder it is
The sweeter the juice in the end I'll drink

Now it is fall of 2010 and I am twenty two years of age. Everything is so strange. Being in school and being a loyal student is difficult as I was just discharged from the hospital. I found it hard to adjust at first and so I felt, "Pressure". There is vocal range that I have to adapt to in singing as I was much use to others tuning, "Pressure".

Pressure

Thoughts of being misplaced

I remember
The death, the hospital beds
I crawled

Feeling pressure

Only knowing through and through
The hospital life
I exceled at it
The world is what I wanted out of
I pried

School is so faint of study
I forgot how to be a student
After being locked up
So many

SHALANDA SHAW

I want friends
I want to feel spectacular
I want to bask in glory
But I am sad today

Sad I tried to end it all at seventeen
Sad because of my journey
Hospital life
I exceled at it

So thoughts of my lost
Is expensive in thought
I want to advance back
My brilliance
At studying
Getting good grades
Becoming a psychologist
Pressure

At a time when feeling upset, angry, frustrated, and sad at the same time I realized my growth from the girl who wanted to kill herself. "I Feel Like..." was developed. I was grateful for a voice.

I Feel Like...

I feel like crying
I feel like shouting
I feel like screaming
I feel like yelling
I hate life
But I don't feel like dying

I can't cry
The tear ducts are dry
I said
I HATE LIFE

I don't need to be rescued
I can FIGHT
Sadness is the prize
This time

I just want to know
Really, really know

HOW DO I MAKE IT?
Through this rough tough time

So...

I feel like crying
I feel like shouting
I feel like screaming
I feel like yelling
I hate life
But I don't feel like dying

Thank you
Thank you, Lord
I have the will to live
After all
I feel like living

The way I carry myself each day and react to another person's negative actions and or words is solidified by the rock I have built my attitude on and not the sandy foundation that is too easy to break down. As a result, my positive outlook is possible, because, "It is the Ground I Walk On". Now having confidence in my singing, I didn't care about what others were thinking.

It is the Ground I Walk On

I

I definitely don't care about having positive thoughts
Because...
Kicked down
Slapped in the face
Hatred of, "I don't care"
Stabbed in the heart
Falling apart
Can't say something without disregard
Care for a jukebox?
Don't you?
Play the songs of my pain
How much further are you going to try to
Rip my kidneys out?
I'm not going to give them to you

Not allowing them to step on my game
The game of life I arduously played
Those passive actions and name calling set to destroy
Yet…
I definitely don't care of your negative thoughts of me
Because ….
While you spit bars of hate
I destroyed them

I
I learned to appreciate me
Learning to not needing you for self esteem
Hi again
I see you
Meet me
Ego Pristine

"So?" is a twisted look taken at mental illnesses. It speaks of one being proud for having his or her illness and not letting it control his or her outlook on life. It simply means that one might have depression or experience some symptoms from an illness, however, so what? Is the question. For it is a part of him or her and he or she is going to make the best of it without letting it define his or her setting. Singing you can do no matter what anyone else thinks, it has to do with confidence and self.

So?

So life goes on the way it is supposed to go
Or so you think
Because here comes
DEPRESSION
ANGER
SUICIDAL THOUGHTS
PHOBIA
MOOD SWINGS
RACING THOUGHTS
PARANAOIA
Knock, knock
They're all at the door
All wanting to come in at the same time
So, what are you going to do?
It's a fight or flight situation

Get help from the psychiatrist or therapist
And come out of denial
As they knock, you kick
Stamp them to the ground
Let them clearly know who is boss
Make it clear they can come back
When they turn into positive thoughts

For simply, you don't deal with the negative
So turn them into mental aspirations
Positive thoughts and attitudes
Day in and Day out

The past is what made me who I am today. It has shaped me, whether they were good or bad actions. I turned out pretty good, I believe. Therefore, as the past experiences are gone they have made me, so they are, "Gone, But Not Faint". The practice helped and sustained my now strengthening voice.

Gone, But Not Faint

Gone, but not faint
The past is distained
The attempt that almost end it
The diagnosis at sixteen
The hatred I felt
The anger that brewed
The voice from the corner of my room
"Shalanda"
I became entangled
Who was going to chaperone?
With fear taking over
My body armor
The so called, "friends" I trusted with my pain
It was such a slap in the face
For no one cares
So silence bites
Yet it is bittersweet
For on my part

There is no will to die
But succeeding in life by trial
Because as I know
Success is
REVENGE
So gone but not faint
Is the past
That builds me again

Having bipolar disorder, at times can be disappointing when going through the motions of symptoms. Therefore wanting to take a lighter eye on the subject I discovered how helpful it would be to look at it as a, "Christmas Present". I now have a gift I can open and play when seem fit, all day, Sing!

Christmas Present

Here's a Christmas Present
I have for you
Time to unwrap it
And make mental illness
Look like it has never been before
COOL

So what if you and I have mood swings
We ride roller coasters for free
Whoosh I am up in the air feeling as a neurotic on beer
Oh man, I am down below, depression has entered the door
High five everyone, there goes the see-saws by the shore

Aren't you just peachy about the next gift,
About what Santa Claus has in store for you?
Aren't you just a little bit curious?
Here it comes
Suicidal thoughts

Oh, thank you, I just love it
For at least I think of my epitaph all day
So it will be perfect
When I tell my family and friends
Before I naturally past any day

Use a little humor when you are down
Mental illness is hard to deal with at times
However, we have a role in this world
Like everyone else does
Embrace your strength
It is not just an illness
Have fun
"You are what you believe"
Lighten up my dear
Remember the secret
Christmas is everyday

PART II

This Is It

Depressed

Depressed I am

Depressed!
I scream
A void so empty
A void so supreme
It eats me up
So I eat food
And drink to fill me up
But
Depressed
The void
I feel it
Who can truly fill it?
No one
But me
Depressed

I am
Depressed
They don't understand
Depressed
I feel it
It has robbed me
So fighting
I want my smile back!
I need to be back on top

Selfish

I tried
Five times that is
Why?
It seemed like the only way out
I said hi to Mr. Death in a coma at seventeen
And he threw me back in the pool
I pressed on the gas
I tried to say hi again
But he ignored me
I spun across the parkway
And I thought it was time
But my Guardian Angel wouldn't let me
A failure, I felt like
But smart, I know I am
Beauty is in my favor
And loved ones are around me
But yet I am
Selfish

It is me that feel the pain
It is me that is drowning
So
Selfish I am
As I have called Mr. Death
Without their approval
Selfish I hope to change
Because that is not the true me

I Hurt

I hurt naturally
I hurt officially
I hurt
I can't explain
I hurt for they don't know me
I hurt
I hurt
Tears fall in vain
Mouth shows vexation
As sadness lurks
I want to scream
I want to shout
I hurt
And I hate that
I hurt
Eyes look on the ground
I hurt
Too much pain

I *hurt*

Why so badly?

I'm just so happy

No one likes misery

And it is written all over me

They avoid

They point

I *hurt*

Why?

PART III

Inspiration

What to Do?

What should I do?
I ask myself
Ask I try to look deep within
I come up empty handed
Sixteen is here again
Friends?
Who are they?
Strangely enough
I don't know
Loneliness!
Hide from them
No one likes Shalanda
They scream it
It is what I hear
Sisters drop their duty
I am alone
I crawl to the light
But it turns darker
The closer I get

Rejection is not old yet
What should I do?
I know
Put a voice to pain
Fellow consumers and I have
Found time and time again
Profound the truth
Give insight to others
It should happen
Very soon

I Beg and I Plead

Listen to me
Brain!
It is you I am talking!
Why are you sick
Why has my happiness fainted?
Why don't you get your chemicals precise?
I beg and I plead
Get rid of my illness
It has bind me
Taken away my smile
And my will to do good
I beg and I plead
Why me?
Change up your nonsense
And set me free
I just want
I just want
My sanity
So brain
It is you I say
Give me back my smile again
I beg and I plead

PART IV

Revenge

August 1, 2012

Revenge

Revenge
It sounds so magnificent
Yet so bare
But daring
I want to get back bipolar disorder
For what it has done to me

I have lost friends and family members
Because of bipolar disorder
I have lost opportunities
Because of bipolar disorder
I tried to kill myself several times
And almost died
Because of bipolar disorder
I lie strapped to a bed with four point restraints
Crying for my mom but she couldn't hear me
As I was in a psychiatric hospital being abused
Because of bipolar disorder
I missed happy days and birthdays
Because of bipolar disorder
I missed jokes
Because of bipolar disorder

So as I think of revenge

The thought gets sweeter
All those things and more
I want to show bipolar disorder
Who can make the higher score?
I dropped out of college
Because of bipolar disorder
But then again
I can write this poem
Because of bipolar disorder
So I smell revenge as sweet success
A poem everyday
Starting from August 1, 2012
I shall rise from the rubbles of pain
By putting it on paper
For Bipolar Disorder will not win anymore
I, Shalanda Shaw, will have the higher score
Bipolar Disorder you will be on paper now

The records of your low blow and disgust
From silly name calling to being stigmatized

Will show my reign of triumph
To overcome and move on
For I am not a label
Nor do you define my life
But I do know my name
And that is Shalanda Shaw
And thriving in life is in my blood type

August 2, 2012

Dare To Dream

Dare to dream

I dare to dream
I dare to dream beyond the tears
I dare to dream beyond the tears, and the pain
I dare to dream beyond the tears, the pain, and the loneliness
I dare to dream beyond the tears, the pain, the loneliness, and the anger
I dare to dream beyond the tears, the pain, the loneliness, the anger, and the depression
I dare to dream beyond the tears, the pain, the loneliness, the anger, the depression, and the suicide attempts

I dare to dream

Dream! Dream! Dream! Dream! Dream!

I am the darn bravest
I went after my dream despite the haters
And fears of failures
I saw it
I reached my goal

I conquered bipolar disorder
I found my balance in handling it and conquered
I am able to inspire others with this book of poetry
And my family finally had an understanding
It took time
But it is here!
The journey was hard and rocky
But who said it was going to be easy
It started with a dream
That was rattled by one or two
But let me tell you this
Don't ever let anyone stop you

I dare you to dream
Dream beyond the pain
Dream beyond the pain and the struggles
Dream beyond the pain and the struggles and who or what
instilled them
And see how sweet success will be

Dream! Dream! Dream! Dream! Dream!

Dream through the tears!

Dream as you fall!

You wipe the tears!

SHALANDA SHAW

You get up!

You plot!

You toil!

You put into action!

Your dream!

You make it!

You shape it!

As real as you want it to be
You give birth to that baby
Keep it in labor as long as you want

Remember it is your dream!

Dream! Dream! Dream! Dream! Dream!

I dream!

You dream!

We all dream!

And Should!

120

Dream! Dream! Dream! Dream! Dream!

Dream Along!

It is!

And

Belongs

To Everyone!

I Want To Share

I want to share

I want to share with
Kindred, that is
Of my new rendezvous
School is no more
And I am going after my goal

See

I called and I left her a message
For her to call me back
I know it was by a long shot
For we have a bad relationship
However, it is not as bad as
Kindred and I would put it
For between us two
It is worse
So, for Kindred and me
I had hope

Kindred and I are not speaking this summer
But that is another book
That bitch tried to get me booked
And told me to go an early grave
"This time make sure you kill yourself!"
That is what the bitch said

Calm down, Shalanda
Calm down

Moving on!

So I was hoping to tell Kindred
That I dropped out of college four days ago
But I guess that relationship was not good also
So yet again I stand alone
Well not exactly
I have mom
And that is a whole
"Only Thinking of Herself"
Doesn't exist anymore
And I have poetry

So I guess
The lesson here
Is that use your strengths
And let the haters fade
They will take up all your strength
Save it!
You need that for success!

Regret

Regret
Who am I to call Kindred a bitch?
She doesn't deserve it
Well maybe she does
Well not
Because if she did
Regret it?
I wouldn't?

Well she called me psycho, crazy, psychotic, bipolar
And oh yeah
A loser
She called me a bitch too
She lied to the police
Said she didn't wish me death
Used my things gladly and abused them
Like they shouldn't be used again
But if I should touch her things
By golly gosh!
It's the coming of Jesus again
Slam doors

Even when I have company
If I walk one way
She walks the other
I like that one though
Because the b….
I mean
The girl was getting out of line
And she had one coming

Anyways she is of my relation
And like it or not
Darn
She gets on my nerves
But I regret calling
Her the b word

So I guess what I am trying to say
Is that the old saying stands true
"Two wrongs cannot make a right"
So while we are all humans
And conflict is natural
Do not let anyone
Allow you to step out of
Your character
Do not let pride stop you
If you are wrong
Acknowledge it

Accept it
Apologize
If they do not want to accept it
Their problem
Move on
Stand tall
And focus
On your goal!

You did your part
In making the wrong, right
It doesn't matter
Who started the fight
It's all about existing in peace
And getting along

This also leads to good energy
And everyone can focus
On the tasks at hand

That reminds me
I have some apologizing to do!

August 5, 2012

My Next Move

What to do next
For I am ill
As I have ups and downs
Hiding from the light
And befriending the dark and night
I have hope
Yet at the same time I want out

So I wonder
What to do?
I still have my dream
But do I have tomorrow?
No more school to look forward to
No one to have long talks with
Just my computer, television, mom, and me
All I have
So I need something for more hope
Something to break free

I discussed this in earlier times
But now I realized
It definitely needs to get done

My next move should be
To a residential home
I will be able to flourish
More independently in life
And accomplish my goals in time

So the ups and downs will continue
For they are in my blood
It's just how I control them
Will be the outcome

Happy

Sad

Glad

Mad

Love life

Hate life

But it still stands
I still want to succeed
And so the actions shall proceed
So my next move I shall make
While still writing!

August 6, 2012

I Lost It

He cursed at me
Like he always does
This time though
I didn't let it go

I was infuriated
I reacted
I blacked out
I don't remember much
But the regret in the dust

A hypocrite I am though
Because out of me
Flying, are curse words
I disrespected my Folk
And my Kin too
Because she was standing there
In disbelief
As I was out of control
Letting anger play the role

Why did he say it?

"…Fuck!…"
That was the word
I don't remember
What else accompanied it
But it hit me
Like a ton of bricks

I was setting for it
Tired of hearing
These curse words
It's one thing to yell
But to tell me a bad word
Heck no!
I am tired of it
Standing up for myself
I did it in a bad way
But I think I got my point across

Folk, this is for you
Stop cursing at me
I lost it
I am sorry
But you need
Better folk training
The lesson learned here
Is that I lost my temper
But I know you're not

Approachable
So if you ever read this
You'll see that
I regret my behavior
So once again
Two wrongs
Cannot make a right
And I acknowledge that
Now I will move on
Despite the fact
You will curse again
I now know
It's best to swallow
The curse words
And curse back
In my head

Dream on Shalanda
Both for folk to stop cursing
And the dream of succeeding
It will one day come true
Demonstrate by leading

August 7, 2012

On My Mind

On my mind
Is hatred
On my mind
Is concern
On my mind
Is boredom
On my mind
Is nerves

On my mind
Is why?
On my mind
Is when?
On my mind
Is what?
On my mind
Is how?

On my mind
Is Kindred
On my mind
Is my future

133

SHALANDA SHAW

On my mind
Is nothing to do
On my mind
Is my Kin

On my mind
Is why she is such a nuisance?
On my mind
Is when will the hate stop?
On my mind
Is what does she get out of all of this?
On my mind
Is how do I repay her for her nonsense?

On my mind
Is frustration
And
Upset

On my mind
I know she does this
On purpose to see me hurt
And out of spite

On my mind
I want to hurt her
Really, really bad

On my mind
Also is to repay her
With what she
Doesn't expect me
To do,
Succeed!

On my mind
I see the frown
And great despair
On her side
Once I achieve success
And prove her wrong
Yep, that's how
I'll repay her

So keep on
It won't be long
I'll get you back

On my mind
I see that I won
The fight
Spite that
Kindred
Say it with me
S-u-c-c-e-s-s

SHALANDA SHAW

Success!
With a smile ☺
Hurray!
For Shalanda!

August 8, 2012

No Funeral Please

I cried
I hollered
I tried to dream my way out

The sharp attack came
From Kindred
I was fragile
I asked her what to do
She slaughtered me
Butchered me
Meat for meat
Word for word
They were the last straws uttered

My last words to her was
"Be a [Kindred] for once!"
And I made up my mind
I must kill myself
There is no hope
No matter what I do
It is just not going to be enough

SHALANDA SHAW

My Kin tried
Yes she did
But like them
Her words hurt
So I must go
And my last wishes is
No funeral please

I do not want
My life to be celebrated
By people who did not love me
Goodbye

Good riddance
On my part
It was your wish for me to go to
After all

Inevitable

I had two choices
Go voluntarily
Or to be taken by the police

As I thought about what
Transpired that day
Being dragged by the police
Like how a pig is dragged by a farmer
When it is time to be killed
Is what I felt like
That is what I wanted

I was done

But then she said,
"I don't want to be embarrassed by
the neighbors seeing the police"
So my heart melted

I showered
Went voluntarily
I was quiet

I was angry

I thought of turning the wheel
No
Others would be at risk
It is just me that wants to die
I thought of jumping out of the car
No
I would make some other guy feel guilty
And put at risk, other lives
It is just me that wants to die

So I gave up the quest
I arrived
Registration!
I am here!
My first fight was to
Resist the wrist band
I was burning with fumes

I told the nurse my story
With tears rolling down my cheeks
My mother interjecting
Suggesting long term care
I was furious
She had to leave for the lobby
I wasn't having it

I asked for four point restraints
"I'm gonna blow up", I said
So they took me to the screeners
Where other patients were packed
Like Sardines
When asked what happened
I said,
"It's my life, and if I want to take it I
should be able to because, it is mine"
But I knew this comment was wrong and stupid
So she gave me two choices
Go voluntarily
Or be committed by a psychiatrist
I'm no fool
Voluntarily of course
It'll be easier
"To Sing To Their Tune"

August 10, 2012

Nothing to Lose

I am at pit bottom

Arrived

Here at the hospital

I cooperate

I cooperate not

I am angry

I am sad

Suicidal?

Still to see

For I am at pit bottom

I feel power

My life is in my own hands

And it is my decision

Whether to let go

Well there's too

They keep giving me

Bad news

I refuse to call my mom

I don't think she cares

Once again

It is just me

So the tears flow
The what if scenarios play
But then
Reality snaps back
It now goes to, what is
I am alone again
No one care to see if I rise
They all are glad I am gone
I wish I can make it permanent

I think about where I would
Like to be in the future
I can't see
It is blurry
I can't see anything
I am at pit bottom
And I have nothing to lose
Mysteries
I want to go where I haven't been before
With nothing to lose
Whether I rise or demolish
I am at pit bottom
The outcome I will relish

No Way Out

I feel trapped
Bogged down
I'm hollering
I'm screaming
But no one is hearing

All I want is a future
I don't want to be dead
But they keep pushing
They were pressures of school
The pressures of life
And no way to adopt to it
It got me wondering
Is it worth living?
I gave up fighting
It was just too hard

I tried talking to the social worker
To brainstorm
What else can be done?
Since I don't want to go back to school
She swept it under the rug
With a WRAP plan packet

I refused it
This is urgent
Reading and filling out
Fifteen pages of paper
Will not help
They are not getting it
I want someone to see
What I do not and did not see
Point it out and set me free
I have no way out otherwise
Darkness is all I see
They are not grasping or understanding me
Please someone,
Help me!

My future, future, future
That's all
That's why I wanted to die
Now let's come up with
Plans to make it brighter
How simpler
Can I make it be?
Without this
I have no way out
Of this disaster
Help me!

*WRAP - Wellness and Recovery Action Plan

August 11, 2012

I'm On a Roll

Anger is clearly present today
As people
Try to press my way
Rude fellow consumers
And supposedly a professional nurse?
I let them have it

"Fuck you,
And go fuck yourself"

I told her to put it on my file
For the doctor to read it
I know she was going to anyway
But I put it in those terms
To rub it in
To show I don't care
For I have, "Nothing to Lose"

I told her she doesn't belong
In the mental health field

"Fuck you, bitch
You belong in the emergency room
to blot cuts"

The bitch was shocked
I wish I could have fucked her up

In here they talk
About using coping skills
Yet this bitch is going to
Give me smirks, attitude
And pass bad remarks?
And yell at me?
And I take it?
I don't think so
Where are her coping skills?

Then I heard her say to the other nurse
"They dish it…"
I didn't even let her finish
So what bitch?
You should dish it too?
NO!
I study in the mental health field
You should smile

And say
How may I help you?
So fuck you!

I first approached her saying please
I don't even know what happened
Someone must have fucked her wrong
That's why I told her to go fuck herself
Maybe she will take my advice
Just saying…hey

Sad, Sad, Sad
I need to work on my anger
For it out of control
Masking hurt with anger
And I am on a negative roll
And it is out of control

August 12, 2012

Realization

I have come to the realization
That school
Is where
I need to be

Dropping out
Made me realize
I was giving up
One of my dreams

It is important to go after
My dream to be a psychologist
Because no matter
What other career paths
I taught of
I felt less hopeless
And more suicidal

So I taught of changes
I could make
To accomplish this factor

Take fewer classes
Don't be ashamed to take breaks
Speak when in need of help
I am in no competition
I will finish college at my own pace

I saw the dream again
Shalanda can be a psychologist
There is no reason to be dead
I'm ready to be thrown back in the world
But my anger?
It still lurks

I believe everything happen for a reason
And I don't regret dropping out of college
Or being suicidal
Because it taught me a lesson
It reminded me of my passion
To want to help others like myself
And how can I be an example
If I give up the dream
Or better yet, dead?

August 13, 2012

Down For One Count

Doctor wants to dictate my life
Putting words in my mouth
I'm fucking mad
I'm fucking pissed
If I could
I would fucking show him
Listing criteria of what
I need to do to leave
Well I have news for him

Nothing comes between me
And my schooling, but me

I am no longer suicidal
But I am for sure angry
With his sarcastic ass
Telling me I make his job easier
Who cares about him and his job?
I just care about my future
And that is to make it to school
This September

He better let me out in time
Because my future is precious
He already has his
So he better do not mess with mine
Down for one count
I hate when the fucking psychiatrists
Want to dictate my whereabouts
Like I'm their child
Down for one count
What the fuck is that all about?

August 14, 2012

Make it

Make it
I can
Make it
I will
Throughout this hospitalization
Throughout life's arduous will

I had a visit with memory today
It was rough at first
Because I lay some things on the table
Tears flow
But a beautiful smile swept in
As, "I'm sorry", followed her guilt

Today I didn't curse
Today I had no arguments

Today I laughed
Today I played cards

Today I read
Flipped pages
Entertained by drama

Of how suicide can horrify
And change lives of those
You leave behind
It was an Irony

Important lesson

I chose the book
Based on the contrasting
Striking purple garden
That pulled me in

Today I saw

I can make it

Today hope rose
And despair fell
Today I saw my future
Again and again

Make it
I can
Make
I will
Make it
It is where I am from
Make it
It is instilled

Apology

Apology I belted
For I was wrong
I cursed her
Through hurt
Covered by anger
Telling her to f herself
How low had I stooped?
How ignorant of me?
Have I no education?
Have I no behavior?

Her apology was well deserved
I was wrong
I disgraced my name
But I must admit
At first I felt proud
But it was false
It was hollow
I was hurt
And as the old saying goes
Two wrongs

Can't lead to the right path
So I acknowledged
I admitted
I said, "I'm sorry"
And it felt good
And even better
She accepted

I hope to do better
And do not continue
To mask hurt with anger
But express it the right way
Because hurting others is not right
It is the cowardly take

Lost

I was shaky of her personality at first
And I liked him
They came to my aid
And sent the pervert to another unit packing
But then I felt something changed
Assured of her ways
And glad to call him psychiatrist
But then came a slap in the face

Lost

I lost respect for them both
The psychiatrist and the social worker
It doesn't matter what I feel, right?
I am just a patient
But it is best that I express
Because he lied
And she said I sabotaged
And called my ordeal a spring
To deny good wealth and happiness
How wrong?
How unprofessional?

Lost

I have lost all respect

So I have been given an ultimatum
Based on lies
Nothing more I despise
But a lie
Nonetheless, I am strong
And this is one for the books
They may have degrees
But they are blinded by words
Not read well
How illiterate
The nurse's report said,
I was restless
Not agitated
Not that I acted up
Restless by medication
That damn doctor raised me up on
My head was cloudy and felt heavy
My eyes felt heavy and puffy
Too much medication!
I used three heating packs
I made a request for an Adavant
And Haldol
After sleep escaped me

So I could be in peace
And this is what he calls acting up
And she calls sabotage
Ha…They don't know me
Downplaying pain and suffering
How disrespectful

Lost

Improvement

I uttered the words through
My lips slowly and carefully
To the treatment team
Made of my Psychiatrist, Social Worker,
A Nurse, And an Art Therapist
I sat in the middle of the circle
All eyes focused on me
I was still mad about
What transpired the day before
Because, "It Takes Over"
For I expressed, "Lost" to
Those that hurt me
And got no response
So further advocating
I had to do

They saw my dismay and disgust
To the social worker
Her word, SABOTAGE
I explained
Was bold in my mind

She apologized
After that took place
I wasn't so hung up

"Now back to the question"
I was able to refocus
How have you improved?
I was asked

Slowly and carefully
I chose my words
Like picking bad seeds
From a pan of corn
But not too slow
Because the pot is boiling
And you need to put them to cook
And the team is waiting
And my every word
They are analyzing

I answered,
I have found new ways
To cope with my anger
Reading
I read two books while I was here
"Butterfly's Child" and "My Sister's Keeper"
I use to hate reading but I like it now

I still have my other coping skill of writing also
I write poetry
I use my words
Instead of acting out
I walk away from others
When they rub me the wrong way
I am no longer suicidal
I no longer have side effects from my medication

I gave an example

My mother visited
And although she was angry
I remained calm
Because of this
She apologized
The visit turned out great

By this time
The psychiatrist was clapping his hands
I don't know if all this was true
Or if it was another edition
Where I,
"Sing To Their Tune"
Improvement?
Maybe

Behave

Behave
It I must do
For the fools
Behave
I must get
On the other side of those locks
Behave
The pervert is working on another unit
Behave
Hard it is
As I think other female patients
Could have and can be victims

Anger prowls
Ready to bite
The next annoying
Or
Attitude prancer
Behave
They must see
A well-mannered Shalanda

I wish I could scream so loud
It would break a window
Behave
They see you as a leader

Behave
I have them fooled
Behave
I always do
Behave
Just a little longer
Behave
The swim will soon be over
Push, Push, Push
Girl
Hold your breath
It is not the Olympics
Trying is acceptable

Anxiety

Anxiety
It is in me
Anxiety
My heart beats
Anxiety
They should have protected me

A pervert is on the loose
They protected his perverted hand
As they allow him to work freely
And defend his ways
When I complain
Excuses they make for him
But I remember vividly

I might have done ECT
But I wish I had done more treatments
Because memory stands still
It plays
Pervert still works
Betrayal of a whole hospital
A victim I am

Robbed of privacy
Robbed of safety
Robbed of treatment
Anxiety
Where is karma
God I call
I need you
Do not let him walk
There are other victims

He may be favored
And so his deed is covered with a smile
But he is wrong
He touched
Every single morning
Covered with sheets over my head
Begging God
He wouldn't come in
But he did
He touched my feet
I was a PTSD victim
Why was he touching me?
Every single morning he worked?
At least twice
I couldn't say anything until now
Because when I told before

He walked in on me naked
They made excuses
It happened again
Coincidence?
So what was I supposed to do?
If I was going to be in the same environment
It was a game of survival
So I pushed it deep, deep, down away
Like it did not happen

Anxiety

My heart beats again

ECT- Electroconvulsive Therapy
PTSD- Post Traumatic Stress Disorder

Breakthrough

She surprised me
"Shalanda, you have visitors"
Hmmm…
I was trapped by interesting drama
Strewn by words
So well written
Eager to know the ending
Smitten by the love story
Yet ravaged and enraged
By arguments that took place
I hesitated to close the book

Who could it be?
It was mom
She said she couldn't make it this weekend
So surprised I was
I smiled
And embraced her with a hug

I let her know
That I felt abandoned
For the first time in a hospitalization

I was alone
The whole family turned their backs
Against me
I even let her know my secret
I was going to spite her
And not go to treatment

She said I would be spiting myself
Which I knew
But I know it was getting back at her too

She said, her not being there was tough love
She didn't mean to
She thinks that trying DBT this time around
Would be life changing
Meanwhile, her cheeks got red
And tears fell

I welled up
As I talked about how abandoned I felt
I call and Kindred did not call back
Folk was yelling at me
When I was complaining about the doctor
Lying about me misbehaving

But, breakthrough
I saw

SHALANDA SHAW

I would talk
And we didn't bark
Breakthrough
There's a bright future
For us two

*DBT- Dialectical Behavior Therapy

A Switch

A surprise
But yet not
Showed itself by erotic fantasies
And a mouth that cannot shut up
I just cannot stop talking

I'm still at the hospital
And I want to be free
So my natural high
A switch I did not see coming
I try to disguise
Mania is here
It showed itself in my pulse to the staff
And my heart beats fast
Ba-bah-ba-bah-ba-ba-bah
It goes
I was asked if it was fast
But I said, no
A switch I like
But it will soon be annoying
A Switch

Hang Out

I thought ahead today
It's Friday!
If I stay home I may feel depressed
So why not hang out with daddy and his friends
At his mechanic shop
Where laughter is non-stop

I did

It was banter all night until after ten
I might hang out next week again

August 22, 2012

Survey?

The service of a well-known Institution went down the drain
But I will give an applause for one thing that remained the
same
The perverted hired hand of one man that still stands
With a nickname that rhymes with Teddy
Starting with the sixth letter of the Alphabet
And they protected remarks of those that make decisions day
to day
Hurray!
Wouldn't you say?
From the despicable food and the ill trained new staff
To the gone smile of the security guards
Who give directions with hand gestures
Everything of this place that has made it once famous
And greet fellow consumers and I
To good health, is gone
Survey?
You say
I don't think so
You know my answer
Poor, poor, poor
Is the outcome

SHALANDA SHAW

I know who did me good
They didn't threaten me or made excuses

Whoever is upstairs
Is lazy
And is not doing enough
For a place to demolish as such
The couches are a disgrace
The excuses made everyday
Come on
It is time to stop and act
I use to brag about this place back in the day
Before I made every effort
To not come back
Because of avoiding the pervert
And now I see I had good reasons
Survey?
I want to say fuck off
And fuck you
But my doctor taught me to do better
So instead
I will say thank you for the pain and suffering
As you see
I used my words
Survey?
Foolish

August 23, 2012

Ready for a Change

Subdued by encouraging words of truth
Inspired by those who have been through it
I entered through the doors resistant
Bolted first with fears
Breakthrough is the armor of anticipation
DBT is here
It is all I have been waiting for
I am ready for a change
I accepted it with both arms
And eager ears
I'm ready for a change
I will be attending
For ten weeks, five days, starting out
with full days 9:30 am to 3:30 pm
No complaints I made about this
That is a difference
I smiled
This is for a better future
I'm ready for a change

Turtling

Turtles are looked down upon
They are seen as slow
Yet this is a characteristic
To their benefit
Yet to mention
Their hard shell
Meant to protect
Turtling
I have to,
Must and will do

Turtling
Slow like the turtle
Grows my patience
As sisters stigmatize
And hurt me like
Blood does not run
Through my veins
Turtling

Turtling
Hard is my spirit
As things happen
To let the words roll off my back
So then I turn to DBT skills
To get through
As I self-right
So it will be harder to relapse
Because I know the quicker I fall
They laugh
Turtling

So my cousin is here to visit
And Kindred is pushing
She disrespecting my existence
I turned to turtling
Turtling

Turtling
It started by not panicking
Taking a few deep breaths
Then reading
Noticing I didn't write my poem
For the day
Inspired
I took it out on paper
Turtling

Turtling
It worked
For we came together
To teach our cousin to ride a bike
An argument I did not spike
I learned to let go
Of the hurt
Turtling

Turtling
So I used my coping skills
Proud that I am in control
I like the feeling
I plan and hope to continue this way
Shalanda takes this piece of cake
Bipolar disorder did not win
Turtling

*DBT-Dialectical Behavior Therapy

August 25, 2012

What I Really Want To Do

What I really want to do
Is call them every nasty name
Known to man
Slap them in their faces
And deem them
To disgrace
Like they did to me

I did not have an ally who was suicidal
And wished my ally death
And told her the next time she makes an attempt
Make sure she kills herself

I did not see my kindred hurting
And willingly ignore it
Then add more to it

I did not have an ally hospitalized
Several times
And did not make effort to call
Or visit

I did not have an ally with bipolar disorder
And call her every stigmatizing word
How cold?

I did not have an ally seeking my help
And companionship because she needed a friend
But I became her foe intentionally

I did not have an ally calling me
And I did not answer the phone, willingly

I did not have an ally sit next to me
And I got up as soon as she sat down

I did not have an ally
Who I try to put down in front of
Extended family and friends
To feel better about myself

I did not have an ally
Who I find all right to borrow
And take her belongings
But yet if she touches mine
It is the coming of God

I did not think that I would end up
Having allies that when I see them
I would lose my smile
I would wish they would soon be gone
And I could escape to some other place

This leads me to
What I really want to do
It is not DBT
It is to fight back dirty
They really hurt me
They did not fight fair
Why were they fighting,
In the first place anyways?
If they had accepted therapy
It would not have been so bad

Stigma
It is bold

I am really, really, really angry
They hurt me
Kindred, I call them
One following the other
Real bitches
Fuck them
And DBT really

SHALANDA SHAW

What I really want to do
Is hurt them!
"It's God"
He gives me a conscience
He saves them

Concern

Waking up this morning
I realize that I miss her
And I miss inside
Not the treatment though
But the routine
Being told what to do
And when to do it
The structure, I guess
This is weird

She was my roommate
And I got to know her a little
But I am afraid that
She is about to subjected
To the shock
ECT
Electroconvulsive Therapy

I did it
Nine treatments
It was supposed to be twelve
But I stopped them

When short term memory
Became a problem
That was the tradeoff though
It helped
I think for the most part
I quit the quest to
Take my life
From those shocks
As it balanced chemicals

So, my fear for her lessened
As there are more pros than cons

As for that place
It is now the weekend
I have my own routine
DBT outpatient
Going there
I do not think so
"Sing To Their Tune"
I would have to do
And that is not pleasing
With a pervert on the lose

Just concerned
I want her to fully recover

Letter to Myself

Dear Shalanda,

Remember I love you
You are a beautiful butterfly
Who have the skills
That has overcome
And will get you through life

Remember to use your copings skills
In battle
Use your words
They are your weapons
Read, play music
Write, write, and write
Poetry
Do not forget
Your dream is to publish
And end stigma
Against mental illness
Do not forget about college
And being that brave psychologist

How about Kin
Your biggest advocate
Keep on loving
And respecting her in every way
She is always there

Also, remember Folk loves you
He just was not raised
To be affectionate

Remember you are intelligent
And good at reasoning
So leave impulsivity at the door
When Kindred
Come ashore

Shalanda, you are beautiful
And you have a lot to look forward to
There is no reason to die
Until God naturally takes you
Fight on
With the giving spirit
I admire in you

Shalanda
Once again
I have to say it
You are beautiful!

August 28, 2012

Always There

She puts up with my mood swings
My repeated nonsense
Highs of annoyance
Bouncing off the walls
Talkative
Lows of depression
Not wanting to leave the bed
Suicide attempts
Threats against self
Self-hatred

Always There

She reminds me of my beauty
Went through Anorexia
Went through PTSD
Went through a short period of hallucinations and delusions

Always There

She stuck through them
Anger lurking

Depression persistent
Racing thoughts looping
Crying spells drooping
Lying dying
Because of trying

Always There

I call her mommy
She shows me unconditional love
I love her too, unconditionally
Naturally it comes
A never-ending relationship
I sometimes forget to show it
As Bipolar disorder binds it

God, thank you
How grateful I am
You brought me to her
Always There
I love her
Always There
Thank God
I love you, Mom
Thank you for always being there
You are a true blessing

Strength

Strength is within me
As I build it
Thinking everything that happen
It happens for a reason
Handed down from the creator
I look up to him
With faith

Strength

Where is it?
Within me
Rooted
Deep down

I access it
In good times and bad
I share it
To maneuver this land

Strength

189

SHALANDA SHAW

I have it
Yet sometimes, I forget
So, Prayer
Reminds me

Strength

A great asset
When I am assertive
But not quite aggressive

Strength

I love it
I admire it in anyone

Strength

It is not a fist
Or a slap in the face
It is expressing me in words
That is intelligent with bass
Strength

I have it
And DBT
Is going to help me
Solidify it

Strength

How great it is to possess it
A ghost is in town

Strength

I see Shalanda as a woman
Who ignores negative comments
And walk away
Head High
No Regrets

Strength

August 30, 2012

Peace

"Livia"
It is sad to say bye
But it was such a good sight to say Hi
Peace
I grant you
As you walk out the door
Onto those streets
With your head high
And remember you have it in you to fight
I know you are feeling anxious
But you have the power within
I am glad to have met you
Our conversations were stinging
And laughter magnificent
Thanks for making me feel comfortable
It is not a bye, bye
But a walk of strength in life
With our hearts connected
With DBT together
Peace
You are ready to fly, "Livia"

Peace

You have it

Peace

"Livia"

Carry on

Peace

Within

August 31, 2012

Smile

What makes me smile?
Are simple things in life
Inspirations of everyday life
I get up in the morning
And I see that my mother is still alive
I have her for a little longer
I have a future to look forward to
If I work for it just a little harder
Dad is here
And he gives me jokes
My sisters try hard
To see me fall on my face
And when I do not give in
The smile is plastered from ear to ear
When I play Jamaican music
That brings back memories of back in the day
Yeah Mon…my sisters, cousins, and I got away with a lot
Mischief, they call it
Hahaha
Getting together with family
And reminiscing about the old days

Looking at old photos and talking about
The stories behind it
How can I forget about romantic and comedic movies?
I just love reality drama
These things make me smile
The list goes on and on
Smile

PART V

Revelation

September 1, 2012

An Understanding

I need an understanding for why I feel like I want to die
And even in the past tried so many times
Bipolar disorder today does not seem like a good reason
It makes me sometimes angry
I need an understanding

September 2, 2012

Failure

A judgment in the roots today
I am not proud as I do some comparing
Of the past and think of the challenges to come
I think
I wonder
I question
A failure I am?
Failure

September 3, 2012

Enjoy

Today is here to be around family
Enjoy their company
And the beautiful surroundings
Labor Day, September third
Jerk chicken, rice and peas, roast fish, baked macaroni and
cheese
Enjoy!

September 4, 2012

Recognition

Recognition
As the tears hit the back of my eye balls
And flow down my face
Recognition
Pervert's actions have affected me in more than one way
Paranoia, anger, sadness
Recognition
Memory plays
Recognition
They have protected his ways
Recognition

September 5, 2012

Couldn't

After "Recognition",
It was an emotional breakdown for me
DBT treatment at a place affiliated with those responsible for
my pain
I couldn't continue
So I was discharged today over the phone
And it is on to the next program
To treat what looks like PTSD
This is what was said by their psychiatrist, not me

Don't

The pain is significant
Emotional I am
Angry I am
Deal with it
I don't want to
Don't

September 7, 2012

Spring into Action

I made an appointment for another program
Nonetheless, with this new revelation
And the problem pervert caused
I realized DBT treatment is the definite solution

I tried to not sell myself short and go back to the DBT
program
For DBT is limited in New Jersey
Meanwhile doing this I became triggered
So I cut the call short
As that Institution has caused me enough pain
Hired a pervert?
And protected his ways?
Fuck them

My future is in my hands now
When it was in their control
They fucked me over
Look what happened?
I probably have PTSD

You know what?
Fuck you

Oh and another thing
Bipolar Disorder should not have been my only diagnosis

September 8, 2012

Party!

Tonight daddy and I host a party
It is his
But I take over
As a music competition I demand
He won as his speakers are louder
And mine has a short
In all it is good fun
I just love my dad
Party!

Really?

Kindred broke my television
When trying to format the picture
My friend, my companion, my one and only
I had an emotional break down
But with this new revelation
I understood it all
My uncle fixed it later
But even during this moment
I had to ask
Shalanda?
Are you doing this?
Really?

September 10, 2012

Revelation

I am in new outpatient program
I will be attending three days a week 10 am to 1 pm
To manage symptoms
This and other things became of my intake
Revelation
I was given three diagnoses
That would be monitored
They were:

1. Bipolar disorder
2. Borderline Personality disorder
3. Post-Traumatic Stress disorder

I was fuming with anger about the third one
I felt robbed and victimized
However, at the same time I felt peace about knowing
About the Second one
And being a master of the first
And having a belief I was in the right place for help
And to be free

The Difference Support Makes

Today was my first day in my new program
Women's group I flock to
For support
My boundaries were violated at twenty
A group of five women understood me
One made me look at things another way
At least the hospital didn't label me "crazy" from get go
They removed the pervert
They made excuses and didn't fire him
I gained from her understanding
Because then it would be their liability
This led to a brighter day
I floated home on out the door at 1pm
High on the clouds
They understood my pain
After all, I wasn't alone
Thank you, God
The difference support makes

I Need to Change

Why do I disrespect my mom?
When she did me no wrong?
Having outbursts?
Taking out my pain on her?
I need to change

September 13, 2012

I Vow

I vow
To treat my mom with respect
To honor her just like how the Bible says
It starts today
And I vow to keep it that way

The Goodness of DBT

So my moods are changing rapidly
And I still have suicidal ideations
I strongly believe it has little to do with my medication
So meeting with my therapist today at program
We came to the conclusion about
The goodness of DBT
We decided to include it in our sessions
So that I can be mindful of my actions
When experiencing mood swings, black and white thinking
And suicidal Ideations
I agreed to keep a daily diary card
Where I record the ratings of my negative self-talk, moods
Quitting urges, moods, and Suicidal Ideations
I also will list skills
I used to combat it all
It was a good session overall

September 15, 2012

Help!

Help!
I need it
Anyone?
Do you hear me?
My thoughts are killing me!
I just want to die!
Help!

Daddy heard me
And he helped me
He spoke words of wisdom
Like never before
Showed affection
Like I was a baby in a basket on the floor
He said, "Shalanda, don't give up, you have to fight."
The word fight stuck with me
It played in my mind
And so I asked him to make me some tea
We started fighting together by watching "Steve Harvey"
Laughing and Commenting
It turned out to be a great night

September 16, 2012

I Fought

The thoughts came again
I fought again
Daddy helped me
We watched "Cops" together
It was a coping skill

September 17, 2012

Calling a Change

So today a change was made to my schedule for program
Due to my rough weekend of calling on death
Calling a change from three half days to five full days was
needed
I hope the skills will also be succeeded

September 18, 2012

Hope

Hope stepped in today
As Kin and I spend time together
We dreamed aloud our thoughts of a better future
I saw them coming through
Hope

September 19, 2012

Rating

Today on a scale of one to ten
Ten being the best
I had a rating of eight
In my way of feeling
Assumptions stepped in
Because of some girls laughing
But I knocked it down immediately
Because rating was up
And I was determined to keep it

September 20, 2012

Worry

I have suicidal ideation
The thoughts have arrived
Floating, churning, taunting, and poking
I want to cry

I love my mom
My greatest fear is that she is going to die
And if she does
According to her
It is my prize
So should I go?
Before I do such a cruel thing?
The logic is I am not capable of such a scrupulous doing
Yet the blame is put
Suicidal ideation arise
Worry is the most
For I worry
Then she worries that I worry

Will a heart attack come from this?
Lord please do not take her?
For I blame me already, like her

Will there ever be a mutual understanding

I want to leave program and go home
Tuck in a corner
Frown, feel the pain
Take the blame
Worry
But not let her know
Because I do not know how else to deal
Can anyone help me?

Process

In process group, I read "Worry"
They helped me to understand
Worry is all natural
And I am not a burden
But my mother feels helpless
She has been my support
And will always be there
My thoughts are just now clouded
By this thing called black thinking
My mom loves me
And I love her too
This is what makes it all difficult
And thus pain ensues

Hang Out

I thought ahead today
It's Friday!
If I stay home I may feel depressed
So why not hang out with daddy and his friends
At the mechanic shop
Where laughter is non-stop

I did

It was banter all night until after ten
I might hang out next week again

September 22, 2012

Party!

My dad host a birthday party for his friend
I was the DJ and I was killing it
Selecting music, I felt the best
The night was wonderful
The party did not end until after three in the morning
I could do it all over again
Party!

September 23, 2012

Remnants

Recovering

Recuperating

Reminiscing

Remembering

Remnants

September 24, 2012

I'm a Failure

I'm a failure
Is the distortion
But I conquered the thought
As I approached my incompletes from college

Technically, I did not drop out of college
I said I would
However, I did not fill out the paperwork to do so

I edit the paper from one of my Psychosocial Rehabilitation
classes
And faced my fear
I read the math teacher's email
Hurray!
He is going to allow me to do the incomplete
I'm a failure?
No
I challenged it
A great feeling

September 25, 2012

Report

I reported to the doctor my prognosis
Doctor, I am doing well
The medications are working
And my skills are no longer lacking
Anxiety have been lowered
I am a little bit paranoid
But mood swings are minor
Everything is on the upper and upper

Thank you

September 26, 2012

Better

I feel better
Much better
On top of the world
Feel like I won the lotto!

September 27, 2012

Chilled

Today I chilled with daddy and his friends again
It became my new norm in the evenings after program
I laughed
And regressed to the days before I turned twelve
I became one of the guys
I felt like one of their friends
However, I knew I was my father's daughter
Therefore I did not cross a certain boundary

September 28, 2012

Safe Haven

I go there five days of the week
Mondays to Fridays
10 am to 3:30 pm
I go to groups
And listen keenly
Give advice
And sometimes share my story
A safe haven
I call it
I wonder if it has been interrupted
I see him
Standing there
Tall and black
I wonder, did the perpetrator send him here?
Could it be true?
Or distorted thinking?
I need to investigate
Because my safe haven has been interrupted
I feel it happened to challenge me

Where it is safe
The best place
So after all
I am safe
I feel vulnerable again
Safe Haven
Save Me!

Comprehending

I now realize to keep up with my illnesses' "score"

Or symptoms

By putting it on paper every day

Was grandiose

I made that decision when I was manic

I now comprehend grandiosity

Which means I am now aware of that or any other little

symptoms

And I nip it in the butt right away

However, keeping a record

Helped me to see

How sneaky the slick is

I see how he moves

And I got a rope on him

I am on the right track

Hurray for me!

September 30, 2012

Rest

So today I decided to rest
I will stop writing a poem everyday
And do what I use to love
Write when I feel like
Forget the pressure
Get rid of the anxiety
And the grandiose idea
Rest

PART VI

Transition

Odd

Oddly enough that guy that triggered me
That I believed the pervert sent to check on me
Did not show up another day for program
This made me stuck to my story
He did not speak
But eat pizza
And watched part of a movie
And he left in the middle of the movie
I wonder why
And he did not show up another day
And he was in all my groups…hmmm?
Distorted?
Odd

But even if it is true
He saw that I am not to be messed with
That is why he left in the middle of the movie
I sat by the door
So I can escape if he wanted to try anything
And I stood my ground and talked in groups

I am strong and smart
I cross my t's and dot my I's
I didn't show any weakness
He should report that
Hahahaha
Odd

Free

Now I feel a freedom like never before
I can say I have suicidal ideations
And I am not sent to the hospital
I record it daily on my daily diary card
If I lied about suicidal Ideations
And on a scale of one to ten how high were they
With my number two diagnosis
This is a norm
So it is accepted
I felt free
After the third week
The lie about suicidal columns had zeros
Because I trusted my therapist
And she understood the norm
And moreover I didn't have a plan
And I was safe
Could life be anymore wonderful?
Free!

Transition

Anger, rage, calm
Sad, rage, depressed
Apathetic, sympathetic, empathetic
Judgmental, caring, understanding
Black thinking, white thinking, grey thinking
Impatient, patient, tolerating

Mommy, Daddy, Sisters
These are all compartmentalizing of my mood swing
I am transitioning
See how much I have changed
Aren't you proud of me?
I have beaten the disorders
And these things I thought that
I am supposed to be stricken with for life
After all
Revenge is mine
Transition
I must admit
I didn't see it coming
I thought my world would end
And several times I attempted
But now I see the middle path

It is not all black or white
It is not all dark
I will be fine
And after all
There is a God
And I am here for a reason
My life has a purpose
Transition
I am worth it
Transition
I will throd on
Transition
I can be whoever I want to be

Trauma

"The Difference Support Makes", helped in my trauma
However, I still have triggers as "Safe Haven" displays
That brief moment helped me
With other encounters

I am strong
I am resilient
I will get through

Acceptance

Two skills in DBT I regress to with almost every problem
Are called "radical acceptance" and "turning the mind"
I learn to accept the emotion as I am feeling it
Accept the situation as it is happening
Don't fight it
Keep making the decision again and again
To switch the mind to what is happening
Acceptance does not deem it good
However, acceptance eases the pain
There is no sense to rebel
But to yield that rope and pull in
For once, I deal with it
Accept the problem, it will eventually fade

Mindful

In DBT I am taught to be mindful
Be aware of the emotions I am feeling
Be aware of when I am feeling that certain emotion
Be aware of my surroundings and how resourceful things
in it could be for my recovery
Mindful
One skill that helps me to be mindful in this way
Is "Opposite to Emotion Action"
This means that I act contradictory to the negative feeling
Or the grandiosity I am feeling
I use my coping skills
The automatic fight I hear from dad when down helps
I try not to be impulsive when anxious and manic
And I try to follow the fifth commandment
Honor thy mother and father
For I want my days to be longer
Upon this land

Image

I have a giving personality
I am very empathetic
I am loving
I am contributive
I am forgiving
I am intelligent
I am understanding
I am caring
I am charismatic
These are qualities
that I have to remember
beyond having an illness
Because recovery does not take a second
It is a process

Body Image

Every now and then
I see my face
Fighting beneath the fat
A little beauty
Glisten here and there
And I want it all back
However, this time I do it
The healthy way
Eat right
However, I don't know
About the exercise
The compliments are just
Flying my way
I keep it up
No all or nothing doing
Moderation will do it
Body image makes me feels good
But "Image", is what makes me glisten

Boundaries

I have rigid boundaries with everyone
Where I do not connect with other people
Except for my Kin and Folk

My Kin and I
Created healthy boundaries to follow
Like when I call her I should talk about the problem
Before crying
Also, I do not call her while I am at program
As of my Folk, we have a mutual understanding
That neither of us will curse at the other
For it is disrespectful

However, going to my outpatient program
I feel like having friends again
Maybe I will make the transition when I go
To school in January
But for now
I will talk to Kin

Gratitude

I am grateful for many things
However, I am most grateful for my mom
Because she recognized I had a "problem"
And sought treatment for me from the age of fourteen
I do not believe that I am saying this
But I am grateful for life
I am grateful that God gave me life
And I am grateful that he guides me through it daily
I am grateful for my sisters and dad, challenging me
When I cross boundaries
And giving me a reality check
I am so grateful for my dad too
For now giving me that automatic thought, "FIGHT"
When I get out of tune
I am grateful for all the doctors and therapists I came across
Those that treated me and lend a helping hand through my
recovery process
I am grateful for my teachers who were patient with me
when I was going through symptoms
I am grateful for consumers who listened to my heartaches
and laughed at my jokes
And provided me with feedback

Like I said I am grateful for many things
I am grateful for anyone and anything that enabled my
recovery process
Gratitude
Newfound glory in my recovery
I love it

Sing!

Sanctified in Holy Ghost

Sanctified in Holy Ghost
Sanctified in Spirit
Lord we here to praise You
Lord we are here to sing and shout
Lord we are here to praise Your name

Sanctified in Holy Ghost
Sanctified in Spirit
Lord we are here to praise You
Lord we are here to sing and shout
Lord we are here to praise Your name

He brought me through the rain-Rain!
He brought me through the storm-Storm!
He brought me through the river-River!
He brought me through them all-All!

So

Sanctified in Holy Ghost
Sanctified in Spirit
Lord we here to praise You
Lord we are here to sing and shout
Lord we are here to praise Your name

Are you ready to be healed?
Are you ready to be cleaned?
Are you ready to be free in Spirit?
Come and praise the Lord

So

Sanctified in Holy Ghost—Sanc Sanc
Sanctified in Holy Ghost-Ghost
Sanctified in Spirit--Spirit
Are you ready to praise the Lord?
We are here to praise Him freely

So

Sanctified in Holy Ghost
Sanctified in
Sanctified in Spirit
Lord we are here to praise Your name
We are here to jump and say
We love Yooooou
AAAAmeen

Thanks

I would like to give thanks to…
God
He saved me
Because I can't kill someone who is supposed to live forever
That is the message He is sending
Thank you Lord
The quest for death has stopped

I would like to give thanks to…
My parents and sisters,
Whether it was getting my medication from the pharmacy
Hiding the medication so I do not overdose
Or staying at home with me
So I wouldn't be alone after dark

I would like to give thanks to…
All hospital staff
That put up with my arguments
Impatience, challenges, and uncomfortable situations I put them in
And thanks for listening to my ridiculous stories, dreams, and aspirations

I would like to give thanks to...
All my peers
That listened to my stories
Nonsense arguments
And received and gave me love

I would like to give thanks to...
All Professors
Who had patience with me in school
Put up with my absence
Understood my illness

I would like to give thanks to...
All extended family members
Who listened to my vents
Loved me through the hard times

I would like to give thanks to...
All Ministers
Who offered me advice
Prayed for me
And spoke words of wisdom

I would like to give thanks to...
To the day programs
Who accommodated my impatience to follow through
program

Who helped my downfalls
And trusted me into graduation with love and adoration
Because you allow me to be me
Shalanda

I would like to give thanks to…
Anyone who I have crossed path with
You may not be in my life right now
But I have grown from it
So thanks

I love you all
Thank you all
May God bless you
And may your path be clear
For there is a way
The silver lining behind that cloud
Whether your words were negative or positive
You helped me find it
Thanks

About the Author

Shalanda Shaw was born and grew up in Jamaica. Shalanda is very smart and started to attend school at the age of two years and three months old. Shalanda had a fair amount of friends, however, at the age of twelve she started to withdraw. She developed an attitude of being dismal towards her siblings, nonetheless, she was very protective of them. Later, it was revealed this happened as a result of the symptoms of bipolar disorder. Shalanda moved to the United States as a teenager where her mother immediately sought help for her. However, for a couple of years Shalanda avoided help by her smartness of telling screeners exactly what they wanted to hear. Shalanda's mother warned the screeners of her daughter's tactics but they didn't listen. Shalanda did this because she thought mental hospitals were exactly as they depicted them in the movies. Therefore, she tried to avoid them at all cost. However, when Shalanda was sixteen, Shalanda's mother mentioned to her that she might have Bipolar Disorder. Shalanda looked it up and she could check off almost and if not everything on the list. Therefore, Shalanda agreed to treatment. This presented a relief to Shalanda, knowing finally a label to her pain.

Through the years diagnoses change but two things remain constant, Shalanda stayed in school and her symptoms of Bipolar disorder persists. Shalanda graduated from a joint program at Middlesex County College and Rutgers in the field of Psychosocial Rehabilitation with an Associate's degree. She also received an award of Outstanding Clinical Performance from the Dean. She is currently attending Kean University and her major is Psychology. Shalanda plans to pursue her Doctorate's degree in order to be a Psychologist.

Printed in the United States
By Bookmasters